POPE
JOHN XXIII

MODERN SPIRITUAL MASTERS
Robert Ellsberg, Series Editor

MODERN SPIRITUAL MASTERS SERIES

POPE
JOHN XXIII

Essential Writings

Selected with an Introduction by
JEAN MAALOUF

ORBIS BOOKS

Maryknoll, New York 10545

Founded in 1970, Orbis Books endeavors to publish works that enlighten the mind, nourish the spirit, and challenge the conscience. The publishing arm of the Maryknoll Fathers and Brothers, Orbis seeks to explore the global dimensions of the Christian faith and mission, to invite dialogue with diverse cultures and religious traditions, and to serve the cause of reconciliation and peace. The books published reflect the views of their authors and do not represent the official position of the Maryknoll Society. To learn more about Maryknoll and Orbis Books, please visit our website at www.maryknoll.org.

Published by Orbis Books, Maryknoll, NY 10545-0308.

Grateful acknowledgment is made to:

Libreria Editrice Vaticana for permission to reprint excerpts from Pope John XXIII's encyclicals, trans. *The Pope Speaks. www.vatican.va*, and from "Christmas Message of Pope John XXIII," December 23, 1959;

Continuum International Publishing Group for permission to reprint excerpts from *The Documents of Vatican II*, Walter M. Abbott S.J., 1966, Geoffrey Chapman; *Pope John XXIII: Shepherd of the Modern World*, by Peter Hebblethwaite; and *Journal of a Soul* by Pope John XXIII, translated by Dorothy White, copyright © 1965, 1980 by Geoffrey Chapman, a division of Cassell Ltd.;

Doubleday, a division of Random House, Inc., for permission to reprint excerpts from *Journal of a Soul* by Pope John XXIII, translated by Dorothy White, copyright © 1965, 1980 by Geoffrey Chapman, a division of Cassell Ltd.;

The McGraw-Hill Companies for permission to reprint excerpts from *John: "The Transitional Pope"* by Ernesto Balducci, trans. Dorothy White (New York: McGraw-Hill Book Company © 1965), and Pope John XXIII, *Letters to His Family,* trans. Dorothy White (New York: McGraw-Hill Book Company © 1970).

Manufactured in the United States of America.

Library of Congress Cataloging-in-Publication Data

John XXIII, Pope, 1881–1963.
   [Selections. 2008]
   Pope John XXIII : essential writings / selected with an introduction by Jean Maalouf.
      p. cm. – (Modern spiritual masters series)
   ISBN 978-1-57075-761-7
   1. John XXIII, Pope, 1881–1963. I. Maalouf, Jean. II. Title.
BX1378.2.J66 2008
282.092 – dc22

                             2007049273

Contents

Sources

AAS   *Acta Apostolicae Sedis.*

ADS   *Aeterna Dei Sapientia.* Encyclical of Pope John XXIII, promulgated on November 11, 1961. Trans. *The Pope Speaks. www.vatican.va.*

APC   *Ad Petri Cathedram.* Encyclical of Pope John XXIII, promulgated on June 29, 1959. Trans. *The Pope Speaks. www.vatican.va.*

CJ   Lawrence Elliott. *I Will Be Called John: A Biography of Pope John XXIII.* New York: Reader's Digest Press and E. P. Dutton, 1973.

CM   "Christmas Message of Pope John XXIII." December 23, 1959. *www.vatican.va.*

DV   *The Documents of Vatican II.* General ed. Walter M. Abbott, S.J. New York: America Press, 1966.

Pope John Convokes the Council.

Pope John's Opening Speech to the Council.

Prayer of Pope John XXIII to the Holy Spirit for the Success of the Ecumenical Council.

GR   *Grata Recordatio.* Encyclical of Pope John XXIII, promulgated on September 26, 1959. Trans. *The Pope Speaks. www.vatican.va.*

IT   Norman Cousins. *The Improbable Triumvirate: John F. Kennedy, Pope John, Nikita Khrushchev.* New York: W. W. Norton, 1972.

JS   Pope John XXIII. *Journal of a Soul.* Trans. Dorothy
        White. New York: McGraw-Hill, 1965.

JTP   Ernesto Balducci. *John: "The Transitional Pope."*
        Trans. Dorothy White. New York and London:
        McGraw-Hill and Burns & Oates, 1965.

LHF   Pope John XXIII. *Letters to His Family.* Trans. Dorothy
        White. New York: McGraw-Hill, 1969.

MM   *Mater et Magistra.* Encyclical of Pope John XXIII,
        promulgated on May 15, 1961. Trans. *The Pope
        Speaks. www.vatican.va.*

OR   *L'Osservatore Romano.*

PA   *Paenitentiam Agere.* Encyclical of Pope John XXIII,
        promulgated on July 1, 1962. Trans. *The Pope Speaks.
        www.vatican.va.*

PD   Pope John XXIII. *Prayers and Devotions from Pope
        John XXIII.* Ed. John P. Donnelly. Trans. Dorothy
        White. New York: Grosset & Dunlap, 1967.

PJS   Peter Hebblethwaite. *Pope John XXIII: Shepherd of the
        Modern World.* Garden City, N.Y.: Doubleday, 1985.

PL   Kurt Klinger, collector. *A Pope Laughs: Stories of
        John XXIII.* Trans. Sally McDevitt Cunneen. New
        York: Holt, Rinehart and Winston, 1963.

PP   *Princeps Pastorum.* Encyclical of Pope John XXIII,
        promulgated on November 26, 1959. Trans. *The Pope
        Speaks. www.vatican.va.*

PSB   Christian Feldman. *Pope John XXIII: A Spiritual
        Biography.* Lives & Legacies Series. Trans. Peter
        Heinegg. New York: Crossroad, 2000.

PT *Pacem in Terris.* Encyclical of Pope John XXIII, promulgated on April 11, 1963. Trans. *The Pope Speaks. www.vatican.va.*

WW Henri Fesquet, collector. *Wit and Wisdom of Good Pope John.* Trans. Salvator Attanasio. New York: P. J. Kenedy & Sons, 1964.

Chronology of Pope John XXIII

1881 November 25. Born at Sotto il Monte (Bergamo), Italy. Angelo Giuseppe was the fourth child in a family of thirteen. Son of Giovanni Battista Roncalli and Marianna Giulia Mazzola. Baptized the same day.

1888 First communion.

1889 Confirmation.

1892 Entered seminary of Bergamo.

1896 Began his *Journal of a Soul.*

1901 Roman seminary. Degree in theology. Beginning of military service.

1903 Ordained deacon on December 18.

1904 Doctorate in sacred theology. Ordained priest on August 10.

1906 Began teaching Church history, then apologetics and patrology.

1916 Military chaplain.

1917 End of his military service. Spiritual director of the seminary at Bergamo.

1921 Appointment to Rome in the service of the Sacred Congregation of Propaganda Fide.

1924 Professor of patrology at the Lateran University.

1925 Apostolic visitor in Bulgaria.

1931   First apostolic delegate to Bulgaria.

1934   Transferred to the Apostolic Delegation for Turkey and Greece.

1935   Death of his father.

1939   Death of his mother.

1944   Nominated apostolic nuncio in France.

1953   Created a cardinal and the patriarch of Venice.

1954   Papal legate at the National Marian Congress in Beirut, Lebanon.

1958   October 25. Entered the conclave after the death of Pope Pius XII on October 9. Elected pope on October 28. Solemn coronation on November 4.

1959   "Christmas Message" on December 23.

        Moto Proprio: Boni Pastoris on February 22.

        First encyclical, *Ad Petri Cathedram,* on June 29.

        Encyclical *Sacerdotii Nostri Primordia* on August 1.

        Encyclical *Grata recordatio* on September 26.

        Encyclical *Princeps Pastorum* on November 28.

1961   "Message for Peace" on September 8.

        Encyclical *Mater et Magistra* on May 15.

        Encyclical *Aeterna Dei Sapientia* on November 11.

        Letter-testament to the Roncalli family on December 3.

        Apostolic letter *Humanae Salutis* on December 25, to announce that the Second Vatican Council was to be called in 1962.

1962   *Motu Proprio: Consilium* on February 2, to announce
        the opening date of the Second Vatican Council. He
        did not live to see its completion in 1965.

        Encyclical *Poenitentiam agere* on July 1.

        Opening speech to the Council on October 11.

1963   Awarded the international Peace Prize of the Eugenio
        Balzan Foundation.

        Encyclical *Pacem in Terris* on April 11.

        Died on June 3.

2000   Beatified by Pope John Paul II on September 3.

Introduction

Wanted: A "Safe" Pope

On June 3, 1963, the eyes of the world were focused on the Vatican. One of the most beloved popes in history was about to die. At the age of eighty-one, Pope John XXIII was ending a reign of only four years, seven months, and six days. People of all faiths and nationalities joined in a united and perhaps unprecedented expression of grief and admiration for the "Good Pope John," as some called him, or "the People's Pope," as some others did. Virtually the whole world felt the loss, and mourned.

Although his papal reign was only a brief moment in history, John XXIII left an indelible mark on his Church and on the world. He knew how to make others listen to him because he was a master at speaking the language of the heart. "He was a man," observed rightly John P. Donnelly, "with whom millions could feel at home — scholars and poets, saints and sinners, farmers and astronauts, the high and mighty, and simple folk" (*PD,* 11). This universal respect and affection could not have been foreseen on October 28, 1958, the day Pope John was elected as the 261st pope of the Roman Catholic Church. The cardinals chose this seventy-seven-year-old man as a caretaker pope who soon would be succeeded by someone more fitting and more capable. On his retreat of 1961, Pope John described the event this way:

> When on October 28, 1958, the cardinals of the Holy Roman Church chose me to assume the supreme responsibility of ruling the universal flock of Jesus Christ, at

15

seventy-seven years of age, everyone was convinced that I would be a provisional and transitional pope. Yet here I am, already on the eve of the fourth year of my pontificate, with an immense program of work in front of me to be carried out before the eyes of the whole world, which is watching and waiting. (*JS*, 303)

Indeed, Pope John surprised everyone. No one could have foreseen the revolution he was to bring about in the papacy, the Church, and the world. His electors wanted a "safe" transitional pope. "In the end," observed Robert Ellsberg,

> he proved to be transitional in quite a different sense. In four and a half years he managed to bridge two utterly different eras in the history of the church. He broke with the fortress mentality of what Karl Rahner called the "Pian era" and initiated a new era of openness and positive dialogue between the church and the modern world.[1]

The conservatives and moderates who had, as a compromise, chosen him as an interim pope were the first to be shocked by the realization that this was not the "safe" pope they had in mind. But by this time, they were stuck with him.

Immediately upon his coronation, Pope John knew what he wanted to do during his reign. He wanted to bring the Church into the twentieth century, but without discarding two thousand years of history. He wanted a Church more Catholic, but less Roman. He wanted a Church that was more caring than controlling, more nourishing than regulating, and more open to a vision founded on faith rather than rooted in ideology. He wanted to implement more justice in all areas of life, without jettisoning all that was related to traditional dogma, doctrine, and discipline. He loved tradition, and more than once he called priests to obedience and caution on the path of social change. But he also wanted to make of this tradition a fruitful guide for the present — not just a treasure to bury in a museum. He had a deep conviction that Catholic tradition and change should originate from the truth of the Gospel. To be truly valid and capable of surviving changing times, every Catholic perspective, whether conservative or progressive, should align itself with the Gospel of Jesus. This was Pope John's deep conviction.

With his Gospel message, Pope John propagated a solid and unshakable orthodox faith. He said at one audience:

> In everyday life one often hears people say: the Church could be more lenient; it could accept a few minor concessions.... Never! The pope can be kind and patient as much as you want; but, given the deplorable realities and the unacceptable omissions, his attitude will be, cost what it may, solid, clear, and unchangeable out of obedience to and respect for the faith. (*PSB*, 153)

This obedience and respect for the Catholic faith originated from his profound understanding of the Gospel truth. Being a man of simple piety and loving kindness, he proposed that all Catholics, whether progressive or conservative, return to the real values of the Gospel and to a Church "without spot or wrinkle." If he was unhappy with some aspects of the Church, he did not just complain by making a list of the wrongs. Rather, with much love and awe, he took the brush of an artist, eager to add a touch of beauty to the already painted masterpiece — a brightness here, a color there, a nuance where it was needed. This is how he explained it in 1959:

> When we have realized this enormous task, eliminating what might from a human point of view be an obstacle on a path we seek to make more easy, we shall present the Church in all her splendor, without spot or wrinkle, and we shall say to all the others who are separated from us, Orthodox, Protestants, etc.: See, brothers, here is the Church of Christ, we have done our best to be true to her. (*OR*, August 10–11, 1959)

It is true that Pope John wanted a Church engaged with the modern world and "[looking] to the future without fear" (*DV*, 712), because the Holy Spirit was active in it and in the world. But it is also true that he could be unyielding when it came to "the sacred deposit of Christian doctrine [that] should be guarded and taught more efficaciously.... The substance of the ancient doctrine of the deposit of faith is one thing, and the way in which it is presented is another" (*DV*, 713, 715). "The breath of newness [John XXIII] brought," confirmed Pope John Paul II, "certainly did not concern doctrine, but rather the way to explain it. His style of speaking and acting was new, as was his friendly approach to ordinary people and to the powerful of the world" ("Homily of Beatification," September 3, 2000).

In a sense, and paradoxically so, Pope John became the innovative traditionalist that the Catholic Church really needed. He did not turn out to be the "safe" pope his electors wanted him to be. Instead, he became a "superb pope" in his own right. But how did he do it?

The Secret of a Peasant Pope

Nothing in his background would indicate that Angelo Battista Roncalli would be the one destined to make his mark not only on his Church but also on the whole world. How was someone born into a sharecropper family at the remote village of Sotto il Monte (Bergamo), Italy, on November 25, 1881, able to become first a papal diplomat in Bulgaria, Turkey, and France for many years, and then move on to become the patriarch of Venice? How was a person of the lowest class in poverty — grandparents, uncles, aunts, and their children were living under the same roof with about twenty-eight mouths to feed (*CJ*, 13) — able to reach the position of the highest authority of the Catholic Church and touch the world with his wisdom, simplicity, and openness? How was so ordinary and

common a man able to do what "extraordinary" persons were
rarely able to do?

There were several secrets behind this. Pope John himself
revealed them this way:

1. "The secret of my ministry is in the crucifix.... Those open
    arms have been the program of my pontificate: they say
    that Christ died for all, for all. No one is excluded from
    his love, from his forgiveness." (*PJS*, 501)

2. "The secret of everything is to let yourself be carried
    by the Lord and to carry the Lord." (John XXIII at his
    coronation)[2]

3. "This is the mystery of my life. Do not look for any other
    explanation. I have always borne in my mind the words of
    St. Gregory of Nazianzen: *Non voluntas nostra sed volun-
    tas Dei pax nostra:* not our own will but the will of God
    is our peace." (*JTP*, 44)

4. "The sublime work, holy and divine, which the pope must
    do for the whole Church, and which the Bishops must
    do each in his own diocese, is to preach the Gospel and
    guide men to their eternal salvation, and all must take care
    not to let any other earthly business prevent or impede or
    disturb this primary task." (*JS*, 308)

5. "Above all, I wish to continue always to render good for
    evil, and in all things to endeavor to prefer the Gospel
    truth to the wiles of human politics." (*JS*, 228)

6. "The maxim 'Know Thyself' suffices for my spiritual seren-
    ity and keeps me on the alert. The secret of my success must
    lie there: in not 'searching into things which are above my
    ability' [Ecclus. 3:22] and in being content to be 'meek
    and humble of heart.' Meekness and humbleness of heart
    give graciousness in receiving, speaking and dealing with

people, and the patience to bear, to pity, to keep silent and
to encourage." (*JS*, 299)

The secret of this poor, unsophisticated, and loving pope is
a return to the basics of Christian life: the Gospel, trusting in
God, and living according to divine will. On this he never com-
promised. He was clear about it. He lived it. His inner riches —
humility, simplicity, poverty, and loving kindness — allowed
him to "feel quite detached from everything, from all thought of
advancement or anything else" (*JS*, 288), giving him the power
"never to ask for anything — positions, money or favors" (*JS*,
343). Pope John believed firmly in the omnipresence of grace,
and he was unshakably convinced that a position of authority is
not about power, but about loving and serving. For theologian
Yves Congar, "This was the secret of [Pope John's] personality:
he loved people more than power."[3] For writer François Mau-
riac, "This great Pope was humble. The Holy Spirit found no
obstacle in him, and for this reason a few months of this pontificate sufficed to make a breach for grace, a breach that will
last for centuries. Through this breach the Holy Spirit will pass,
and there will be nothing to stop him" (quoted in *JTP*, 28). And
for Henri Fesquet, "The secret of [Pope John's] success is the
mystery of a soul, the mystery of grace itself" (*WW*, 23).

The grace of being transparent to God, inflamed by the Holy
Spirit, and completely surrendered to God's will makes one
move mountains, indeed.

"Holy I Must and Will Be"

On his retreat of 1961, Pope John wrote: "Everyone calls
me 'Holy Father,' and holy I must and will be" (*JS*, 303).
His unqualified determination toward this goal seems to have
constantly dictated his words and deeds.

For sixty-seven years, Pope John kept a diary, which became
in a sense his autobiography: *Journal of a Soul.* Throughout

its pages, the reader is struck by his lifelong quest to become a saint. The peasant boy, at the starting point of the *Journal*, and the most powerful spiritual leader, at the conclusion, have one thing in common: an earnest dedication to a life of spiritual perfection and a deep desire for holiness. This holiness did not remain for him just an ideal or a theoretical principle. He took practical steps toward achieving this goal.

In 1895, when he was only fourteen, he opened his *Journal* with "Rules of life to be observed by young men who wish to make progress in the life of piety and study" (*JS*, 4). He described what to do every day, every week, every month, every year, and at all times detailing all the spiritual practices. Five years later, he felt determined to keep going forward, trying to have "the spirit of union with Jesus, the spirit of recollection in his Heart from my first awakening in the morning until I close my eyes at night and, if possible, also during my dreams at night" (*JS*, 75). Then he added that he wanted to practice "tranquility, calm, cheerfulness, good manners, never a cross word with anyone, no excited speech, but simplicity, cordiality, sincerity without cowardice — no flabbiness" (*JS*, 75).

Then, in 1903, there was an evolution in his way of thinking about holiness. He admitted that he used to think that to imitate a saint it was necessary to do exactly what that saint had done. Now he realized that in real life he could never do exactly what that saint had or had not done. "The method was wrong," he wrote. "From the saints I must take the substance, not the accidents, of their virtues.... God desires us to follow the examples of the saints by absorbing the vital sap of their virtues and turning it into our own life-blood, adapting it to our own individual capacities and particular circumstances" (*JS*, 107).

In 1904 he resolved to be more careful in his spiritual practice. He decided that the time before Mass would be consecrated to exclusively spiritual thoughts and occupations like prayer, spiritual reading, meditation, the recital of the Divine Office. As part of his daily practice, he decided to pay more attention to examining his conscience and visiting the Blessed Sacrament. He also decided to obey all the rules of the seminary and not miss the monthly day of recollection. And he felt that "in all things there must be humility, great spiritual fervor, mildness and courtesy toward everyone, continual cheerfulness and serenity of mind and heart" (*JS*, 163).

The sources he used as means for his spiritual journey were quite traditional: the Scriptures, the Fathers of the Church, the breviary, the liturgy, the lives of the saints (his favorite ones were Joseph, John the Baptist, John the Evangelist, Francis de Sales), the *Imitation of Christ* and other spiritual classics, the rosary and other popular devotions, weekly confession, annual retreats, and works of mercy.

When he was fifty-three, he asked himself if he could do anything more in order to make himself holy, and his answer was to "continue under obedience as you are now; do your ordinary things, day after day, without over-anxiety, without ostentation, but always trying to do them with greater fervor and perfection" (*JS*, 222).

At the age of sixty-seven he found that "the surest way to make myself holy and to succeed in the service of the Holy See lies in the constant effort to reduce everything, principles, aims, position, business, to the utmost simplicity and tranquility; I must always take care to strip my vines of all useless foliage and spreading tendrils, and concentrate on what is truth, justice and charity, above all charity" (*JS*, 270).

At the age of seventy-two, when he became patriarch of Venice, he wrote: "In the few years I have still to live, *I want to be a holy pastor,* in the full sense of the word.... 'So help me God'" (*JS*, 283).

In 1961, when he was already the pope and was eighty years old, he reflected on his journey to holiness in terms of humility and constant striving to perfection. He realized that the quest for holiness was an unceasing journey. He wrote:

I am very far from attaining this holiness in fact, although my desire and will to succeed in this are whole-hearted and determined. This particular way of sanctification, which is the right way for me, has once again been shown to me here at Castel Gandolfo, in a passage in a book and in a picture.

The passage I came across unexpectedly in a little volume: *La perfezione cristiana: Pagine di ascetica* by Antonio Rosmini, page 591: "In what does sanctity consist? ... Reflect on this thought, that sanctity consists in being willing to be opposed and humiliated, rightly or wrongly; in being willing to obey; in being willing to wait, with perfect serenity; in doing the will of your Superiors without regard for your own will; in acknowledging all the benefits you receive and your own unworthiness; in feeling a great gratitude to others, and especially to God's ministers; in sincere love; in tranquility, resignation, gentleness and the desire to do good to all, and in unceasing work. I am about to leave and can say no more, but this is enough" (Stresa, September 6, 1840).

I find it comforting to note that these are simply the applications of my own special motto, which I took from Baronius: *Obedientia et Pax*. Jesus, this shows me that you are always with me! I thank you for this doctrine, which seems to follow me wherever I go. (*JS*, 303–4)

Pope John proved that real "greatness" and true "success" are not necessarily defined in secular terms. It is not by accumulation of things and power and prestige that one is great. It is by subtraction. The "I am nothing" (*JS*, 291), by which he repeatedly described himself, points to the One who is in charge in his life. He is clear about it: "In the eyes of the Lord I am a sinner and nothing but dust: I live by the mercy of Jesus, to whom I owe everything and from whom I expect everything" (*JS*, 307).

Such a conviction led Pope John to have a providential view of history under the guidance of the Holy Spirit. Rooted in his deep faith, his complete trust in God provided him with a remarkable sense of joy and optimism — some even called it "naïveté" — that empowered him to do unusual things and to breed circumstances no one could have imagined.

"The Good Shepherd"

On November 4, 1958, the day of his coronation, Pope John defined the way he wanted to be a pope: as pastor rather than as expert administrator, as priest rather than as skilled prelate, as servant rather than as politician sovereign. People, he said, must not look to him for the "statesman, diplomat, scientist or social organizer, but for the shepherd" (PD, 8), the universal shepherd and the "servant of the servants of God." He saw the "Peter" role in him as of someone who strengthens, encourages, motivates, and supports his brothers.

Pope John wanted to reach out to everyone, Catholic and non-Catholic. He did not wait long before he broke with Vatican traditions and went to visit orphanages, jails, schools, convalescent homes, educational and charitable institutions, local parishes, and hospitals a great number of times — 139 times, according to some sources. These same sources also say that he welcomed more rulers than any previous pope. He received the first Greek Orthodox sovereign to visit the pope since the days of the last Byzantine emperor, the first archbishop of Canterbury since the fourteenth century, the first chief prelate of the U.S. Episcopal Church, the first moderator of the Scottish Kirk, the first Shinto high priest, and many others. In his retreat of 1959 he wrote:

Since the Lord chose me, unworthy as I am, for this great service, I feel I have no longer any special ties in this life,

no family, no earthly country or nation, nor any particular preferences with regard to studies or projects, even
good ones. Now, more than ever, I see myself only as the
humble and unworthy servant of God and servant of the
servants of God. The whole world is my family. This sense
of belonging to everyone must give character and vigor to
my mind, my heart and my actions. (*JS*, 298–99)

It goes without saying that Pope John must constantly have
had in mind the image of the Good Shepherd of the Gospel and
the instruction of Jesus to Simon Peter, "Feed my sheep" (John
21:15–17).

But who were these sheep?

To Pope John, the Church was not a "for-members-only"
club that was reserved for the elites. He felt that the Church
must bring Christ to the world and bring the world to Christ.
In this context it was remarkable to hear what Pope John said
just a few days before his death. According to his secretary Loris
Capovilla the pope said: "Today more than ever, and certainly
more than in the last few centuries, we are oriented to serving
humanity as such, not just Catholics, to defending first of all
and everywhere the rights of the human person and not just
those of the Catholic Church" (*PSB*, 177). The Church must
follow men and women wherever they are in life — to the sky if
they fly there or to the mud if they are stuck there. Salvation is
its mission, first and foremost. This is why Pope John, knowing
the truth of human nature, was realistic in seeing human beings not only as "what they ought to be," but also "as they are
here and now." When theological issues arose, he preferred to
count more on the inspiration he had from the Holy Spirit than
on the sophisticated reasoning of theologians. Here it is fair to
say that, even if he held theology in great esteem, he had at the
same time a certain distrust for theologians. He once remarked
to an Anglican "observer": "It is the theologians who have got

us into this difficulty, now it is for the ordinary Christians, like you and me, to get us out of it" (*JTP*, 122).

For Pope John, real life took precedence over theoretical definitions. And so, when confronted by error, he favored the power of positive example more than a syllabus of untruths. He saw that charity might be more efficient than "correctness," and mercy more healing than "strictness." He saw that "often errors vanish as quickly as they arise, like fog before sun" (*DV*, 716). And he continued: "The Church has always opposed these errors. Frequently she has condemned them with the greatest severity. Nowadays, however, the Spouse of Christ prefers to make use of the medicine of mercy rather than that of severity. She considers that she meets the needs of the present day by demonstrating the validity of her teaching rather than by condemnations" (ibid.). It was reported that during the preparation of the Second Vatican Council, he took a ruler and measured the page of condemnations and said: "Seven inches of condemnations and one of praise: is that the way to talk to the modern world?" (*PJS*, 414). In a very practical way, he took to heart the advice of St. Bernard of Clairvaux: "To notice everything, turn a blind eye to much and correct a few things" (*PJS*, 422).

But this kind of perception did not draw unanimous consent. The Roman curia, which is the central administrative body of the Catholic Church, was the first to question the validity of Pope John's reasoning.

At the time of Pope John's pontificate, the curia was in full control of every move in the Church, fully enjoying the dictum, *Roma locuta est; causa finita est* (Rome has spoken; the matter is settled). These mostly aging Italian cardinals seemed opposed to the modern world and were suspicious of a pope who initiated change through the Council. Cardinal Alfredo Ottaviani, who was the head of the Holy Office at that time, described best this attitude. He was heard to have said: "I pray to God that I may die before the end of the Council — in that way I can die Catholic" (*PJS*, 414).

Pope John knew exactly what was going on and what he was facing. Speaking of the curial fathers, he said: "They are zealous men, but it is not they who rule the Church. The post is mine" (*CJ*, 284). He knew how the curia worked, and he also knew how to deal efficiently with it and not waste time trying to use it as an instrument for change. For that purpose he turned to the two ancient instruments available to him: encyclicals and a universal council. He sensed that the time was ripe for internal renewal in the Church and that it was his mission to seize the moment. Later on, just a few days before his death, he confided, as his secretary Loris Capovilla recorded, that:

> today's situation, the challenges of the last fifty years and a more profound understanding of the faith have brought us face to face with new realities, as I said in my inaugural address to the Council. It is not the Gospel that has changed. No, we are the ones who are just now beginning to understand it better. Anyone who has lived a fairly long life, anyone who at the beginning of this century confronted the challenges of a social activity that dealt with the entire person, anyone who, like me, spent twenty years in the East and eight in France and by so doing could compare different cultures with one another, such a person knows that the moment has come to recognize the signs of the time, to seize the possibilities they offer and to look far ahead. (*PSB*, 177)

A Breath of Fresh Air

From the perspective of certain conservatives, the First Vatican Council of 1870, in defining the doctrine of papal infallibility, had obviated the need for further councils. What purpose could another council serve? When this question was put to Pope John, he walked over to the window, opened it, and said: "What do we intend to do? We intend to let in a little fresh air" (see *IT,* 61, and *CJ,* 289). This "little fresh air" became, in just a little while, a deep breath of the Holy Spirit.

Pope John's instincts told him that if you want fresh water, you must keep it running. Inertia and resistance to change produce undesirable results. This is how G. K. Chesterton, in his subtle way, described such a phenomenon:

> Conservatism is based upon the idea that if you leave things alone you leave them as they are. But you do not. If you leave a thing alone you leave it to a torrent of changes. If you leave a white post alone it will soon be a black post. If you particularly want it to be white you must be always painting it again; that is, you must be always having a revolution. Briefly, if you want the old white post you must have a new white post.[4]

Tradition must always be revised if it is to be honored. And the best way to revise it is to go back to its origins — the source — and find out why it is there in the first place. Pope John knew that the Church should always be in a state of renewal, and the way to achieve this, paradoxically, was to go back to the source — the original inspiration. This is exactly what he wanted to achieve with the Council he convened: renewal from the original source.

By opening the Second Vatican Council — a very rare event considering there have been only twenty ecumenical councils in the Church's history — Pope John provided a climate for a new way of thinking and triggered unstoppable ideas and forces that affected not only Catholics and other Christians, but the entire world. Some people even called the event a "revolution" in Christianity.

In any case, Pope John called for a spirit of *aggiornamento* — "updating" or renewal — that would affect the life and worship of every Catholic and, by so doing, would help prepare the way for the distant end that is the unity among all Christians, and the conversion of all nations to the Gospel message. On one occasion Pope John confided to his listeners how he saw the role of the Church in the world: "It is important to always keep moving and not to rest on traditional paths. We have to keep seeking new contacts, and to always be receptive for the legitimate challenges of the time in which we are called to live, so that Christ may be proclaimed and recognized in every way" (*PSB*, 11).

Back to Basics

Pope John's call was essentially a call "back to basics." He reminded everyone that the ideal of Christian life is supposed to be measured by the pure standard of the Gospel. In a letter to his nephew Battista, he unequivocally wrote: "All knowledge, human or divine, takes light from the Gospel, the Gospel pure and simple as St. Francis of Assisi taught it" (*LHF*, 623). Since the Gospel is the process that brings the reality of God and the reality of being human to the fullness of life, one should always see things with the eyes of the Gospel.

In the midst of the huge changes in science, economics, psychology, social sciences, ethics, and politics that swept the twentieth century, Pope John wanted to show that the Gospel remains relevant and adequate to answer our curious minds and thirsty hearts. He refused to concede that the animosity and hypocrisy that sometimes hang over some attitudes and actions of Christians equate with the Gospel. He saw that our divisions and quarrels are there because we practically repudiate God by failing to live the Gospel.

Pope John was eager to "[bring] the modern world into contact with the vivifying and perennial energies of the gospel" (*DV*, 703). "Our life," he wrote to his brother Giovanni, "is sure of every success provided that we follow the teaching of the Gospel which tells us to have patience, to return good for evil, to forgive, and ... to pass over many things in silence. When the final account is made we shall see which are the things of real benefit to us" (*LHF,* 387).

Pope John was obsessed with the Gospel, and he wanted to communicate its message to others in a way they could understand it. He wanted the Gospel to permeate their consciousness, their minds and hearts, their decisions and actions — their entire lives. Only such a deep transformation was capable of bringing about a new order of human relationships.

The term *convivenza* — the Italian term that means co-existing — comes closest to what Pope John wanted to convey when he talked about human relationships. As explained by Bernard R. Bonnot, it means intimacy, not just togetherness, and communion rather than just societal living. It implies "real coordination and integration, a fraternity of love."[5]

Convivenza was experienced by Pope John, long before he started to talk about it. It was grounded in his own peasant family at Sotto il Monte, where, as a child, he lived a well-bonded family life. Later, as pope, he wanted to extend this experience not only to the Church, but to the whole world as well. "The whole world is my family" (*JS,* 299), he said in 1959. Indeed, he delivered what he said by providing to the world at large a sense of human family, regardless of faith. And he did not consider himself superior to any other person. Norman Cousins reported an audience he had with Pope John this way:

> Monsignor Cardinale and I followed the pope into his oak-paneled study. No sooner had I entered the room than the Pope turned to me. "We have much to talk about," he said. "Just remember, I'm an ordinary man; I have two eyes, a nose — a very large nose — a mouth, two ears, and so forth. Even so, people sometimes remain rigid and uncommunicative when they talk to me. You must feel completely relaxed. We will talk as man to man." He smiled. (*IT,* 62)

Pope John loved people. As early as the first days of his pontificate, this pope stopped taking his meals alone. To those who objected, he noted that he could find no text in the Bible that required him to take his meals alone, and that Jesus, too, liked to eat with others. His openness to all, his desire to build bridges, his deep respect for everyone made him "a genius in human relationships" (*IT,* 60). Few would dispute this self-estimation by the pope in his later years:

> May everyone be able to say of me that I have never sowed dissension and mistrust. That I have never grieved any immortal soul by engendering suspicion or fear; that I have been frank, loyal, trusting; that I have looked into the eyes of others with brotherly sympathy, even into those of persons who do not share my ideals, so as not to hinder the realization, in its season, of the great commandment of Jesus: *Ut unum sint!* [That all may be one].[6]

Creating True Peace

The first night after his election as pope, John XXIII couldn't sleep. "I spent the entire night in prayer," he told the French author Henri Daniel-Rops. "It was such a burden that I now had, such a weight. But the Lord wished it" (*CJ,* 253). Then, the next morning, following the Mass for the cardinals, he delivered an appeal for peace — an appeal addressed directly to the rulers of nations. He said:

> Why is it that our divisions and disagreements are still not able to be settled on the basis of fairness? Why should the resources of human ingenuity and the riches of nations turn so often to the production of arms — pernicious instruments of death and destruction — instead of improving the welfare of all classes of citizens, and particularly of those who live in poverty?... Take action, boldly and with confidence, and may heaven's inspiration be given to

each of you, and may divine aid be yours. Look at the
people entrusted to you and listen to their voices. What
do they seek? What do they implore of you? Not these
new monstrous instruments of war which our times have
produced and which can annihilate us all — not these, but
peace. (*CJ,* 253)

With this appeal, Pope John wanted to underscore the great urgency of world peace. This was a primary and essential focus
of his pontificate, and he wanted to do whatever he could to
promote it. He wanted to use his papacy to make the Church
an efficient instrument in the cause of unity and peace, and for
this cause he was not afraid to talk to anyone. He once said in
a conversation with Norman Cousins:

The Russian people are a very wonderful people. We must
not give up on them because we do not like their political system. They have a deep spiritual heritage. This they
have not lost. We can talk to them. Right now we have to
talk to them. We must always try to speak to the good in
people. Nothing can be lost by trying. Everything can be
lost if men do not find some way to work together to save
the peace. I am not afraid to talk to anyone about peace on
earth. If Mr. Khrushchev were sitting right where you are
sitting now, I don't think I would feel uneasy or awkward
in talking to him. (*IT,* 63)

Pope John's "unorthodox" intervention in the Cuba missile
crisis of 1962, for example, was remarkable. When he saw
the world on the brink of possible annihilation, he was able
to reach out to Chairman Nikita Khrushchev and President
John F. Kennedy to discuss backing off without losing face. He
asked the statesmen to exercise the greatest restraint and to do
whatever possible to reduce the terrible tension.

On October 26, 1962, a sea of radio microphones carried the
uncompromising papal voice: "Hear the anguished cry which

rises to heaven from every corner of the earth, from innocent children to old men, from the people in cities and villages: Peace! Peace!" (*CJ*, 307–8).

If Chairman Khrushchev and President Kennedy had to go against powerful cross-currents within their own countries, Pope John had to break with papal tradition in order to intervene directly in a world crisis. Even more untraditional was his desire to establish contacts with the Communist world power. He felt that any means should be used to help bring peace on earth.

He followed this gesture with an encyclical about peace, which he addressed, not only to the clergy and the Catholic world, as was the custom, but also to all people of good will.

Pacem in Terris (Peace on Earth) was Pope John's last encyclical letter — a moving testament. It was issued on April 11, 1963, just a few weeks before he died on June 3. This encyclical can perhaps be considered not only his last message to the world but also a basic document on what a Christian political philosophy looks like. This encyclical starts with a short description of the marvelous order of the universe, given by God but disrupted by sin. It then develops into five sections: (1) order between men, (2) relations between individuals and the public authorities, (3) relationships between states, (4) relationships of men and of political communities with the world community, (5) pastoral exhortations. It argues for the peace that is dependent upon a just world order, mutual trust, and honest treaties. It talks about elementary human rights including the right of "being able to worship God in accordance with the right dictates of [a person's] own conscience, and to profess his religion both in private and in public" (*PT*, 14).

This visionary encyclical on world peace is openly optimistic. It assumes that peaceful coexistence, based on trust instead of fear among nations, is possible and urgent. This would make the stockpiles of weapons unnecessary and an agreement on disarmament reachable.

Brilliantly reasoned, boldly conceived, and gently engaging, *Pacem in Terris* can be seen as a blueprint for a world community in which people of different religious, cultural, and political persuasions could have a better understanding of their rights and duties and the common good, and could live in harmony, justice, security, freedom, truth, mutual respect, and love.

In his message for World Peace Day, January 1, 2003, Pope John Paul II recalled: "With his confidence in the goodness he believed could be found in every human person, Pope John XXIII called the entire world to a nobler vision of public life and public authority, even as he boldly challenged the world to think beyond its present state of disorder to new forms of international order commensurate with human dignity."[7]

Pope John's visionary agenda for peace remains a challenge for everyone — statespersons, spiritual and political leaders, as well as ordinary citizens. At a time when violence threatens civilizations, every one of us is called, in the footsteps of Pope John, to defend human rights, to aid the poor, to recognize and support global institutions, and to try tirelessly to build a culture of peace.

Lessons from a Master

To spend time with Pope John XXIII, even through his writings, is to come away feeling more optimistic, more hopeful, more open to the Holy Spirit. What practical lessons can one draw from this modern master, whose deep desire was to be our "brother," and who was often described as the "shepherd to the modern world"?

There is no shortage of lessons that can be taken from this modern master. Let us consider the following fifteen guidelines.

1. *Total abandonment to God's will.* Throughout his life and ministry, Pope John kept repeating his resolve to surrender to God's will. "All my endeavor is to do God's will at all times," he

once wrote to his niece Giuseppina (*LHF,* 810). "I must abandon myself completely," he wrote in his journal, "to the will of
the Lord and desire to live for nothing else but the apostolate
and the faithful service of the Church" (*JS,* 259). Since he was
convinced that God takes care of everything and that included
the future, Pope John did not work for positions and did nothing to become a pope. "I accepted this service," he wrote, "in
pure obedience to the Lord's will, conveyed to me through the
voice of the Sacred College of Cardinals in conclave" (*JS,* 313),
and "I have accepted with simplicity the honor and the burden of the pontificate, with the joy of being able to say that I
did nothing to obtain it, absolutely nothing" (*JS,* 325). Indeed,
Pope John's providential view of history — his own history as
well as world history — directed his whole life and especially
his ecclesiastical career.

2. *Redefining and reordering life's priorities according to
"what matters most."* Pope John wrote: "What matters most
in life is: our blessed Jesus Christ, his holy Church, his Gospel,
and in the Gospel above all else the Our Father according to
the mind and heart of Jesus, and the truth and goodness of his
Gospel" (*JS,* 344). It is imperative to preach, and live according
to, the Gospel. The Gospel is above social parties, human inter-
pretations and judgments, personal opinions, and the various
ways of thinking and feeling (see *JS,* 307–8). We should "judge
what is happening . . . in the light of what the Gospel teaches us"
(*JS,* 260). "To all [God] has made clear the rules which govern
human society: they are all to be found in the Gospel" (*JS,* 238).
"The Gospel contains the fullness of holiness" (*PD,* 212). The
Gospel shapes people's values. The Gospel is the dynamic that
gives substance, form, and meaning to Christian life.

3. *Living a life of prayer.* Pope John was a man of prayer.
He used to get up early in the morning — around four o'clock,
sometimes even earlier — and pray the Church's morning prayer.
"Prayer goes so well at first light, when everything is quiet,"
he once said (*PSB,* 113). Throughout his retreats, he very often

expressed his longing of union with God. "I renew my resolutions concerning the life of prayer and union with God" (*JS*, 213). "I must, I will, become increasingly a man of intense prayer" (*JS*, 210). "My day must be one long prayer: prayer is the breath of my life" (*JS*, 283). Prayer is key in Christian life.

4. *Being determined to be holy.* Repeatedly Pope John expressed his unshakable resolve to be holy. For example, he wrote in his journal: "I must be holy at all costs" (*JS*, 94). "My obligation to aim at sanctification at all costs must be ever present in my mind....I must remember it at every moment, from when I first open my eyes to the morning light till I close them in sleep at night" (*JS*, 111). "I renew my resolution to make myself really holy" (*JS*, 75). "My only wish is that my life should end in a holy manner" (*JS*, 280). "Everyone calls me 'Holy Father,' and holy I must and will be" (*JS*, 303). This universal call to holiness was underscored by the Second Vatican Council (see especially *Lumen Gentium*, nos. 40–41).

5. *Living a life of simplicity and humility.* The different distinguished positions of his career — representative of the Holy See for many years and in different countries, then becoming the patriarch of Venice, then the pope with all the power and honor and prestige a pope can have — could have been opportunities used for personal advantage. But Pope John did not succumb to such temptations. He always wanted to be, and was indeed, on the side of simplicity and humility. He would say, for example: "Humble and unpretentious as I know myself to be, I was always warmly welcomed wherever I went" (*JS*, 312). "I feel I am under obedience in all things, and I have noticed that this disposition, in great things and in small, gives me, unworthy as I am, a strength of daring simplicity, so wholly evangelical in its nature that it demands and obtains universal respect and edifies many" (*JS*, 299). "The older I grow the more clearly I perceive the dignity and the winning beauty of simplicity in thought, conduct, and speech: a desire to simplify all that is complicated and to treat everything with the greatest naturalness and clarity,

without wrapping things up in trimmings and artificial turns of thought and phrase" (*JS*, 278–79). "Born poor...I am particularly happy to die poor.... [Poverty] has strengthened me in my resolve never to ask for anything — positions, money or favors — never, either for myself or for my relations and friends" (*JS*, 343). When one has a true sense of history, as Pope John had, one cannot but make of humility a central part of life.

6. *Living by what we preach.* Obviously, it is easier to preach the Gospel than to live it, and it is more convenient to insist on the expectations we have of others than of ourselves. Pope John taught that we should first live what we preach. He said, for example: "We cannot always require others to observe the Church's teaching on social justice if we do not apply it in our domain. The Church must take the lead in social justice by its own example" (*PL*, 48). In social justice and in many other areas, Pope John offered a living example, for he succeeded in identifying the teaching of the offices he occupied throughout the years with the teaching of his life. He was a true Christian and a great teacher. His teaching was the image of his life, and his life was the incarnation of his teaching. And this was done without compromises because he always "[endeavored] to prefer the Gospel truth to the wiles of human politics" (*JS*, 228).

7. *Living a life of goodness and kindness.* Known affectionately as "good Pope John," and called often by the media "the most loved pope in history," Pope John reminds us of the goodness and kindness of a loving father, mother, or grandparent. This was one good reason for everyone — especially for those who did not feel loved by the Church — to feel close to him and be touched by his goodness. His strategy was not to fight enemies but to win them over by love. He always tried to conquer evil with good. When goodness is real, it makes the heart reasonable. This is what a father does. Pope John wanted always to relate to his flock, not as a CEO relates to his employees or clients, but as a father relates to his family. Goodness is the fruit

of a single-hearted love for God and neighbor. "My dealing with others," he wrote, "must always be marked with dignity, simplicity, and kindness, a radiant and serene kindness" (*JS*, 213). Pope John Paul II said in his homily for the beatification of Pope John XXIII on September 3, 2000: "[Pope John XXIII] impressed the world with the friendliness of his manner which radiated the remarkable goodness of his soul."

8. *Recognizing the necessity to continue to bring the Church up to date.* In his opening speech to the Second Vatican Council, Pope John clearly stated: "The Church should never depart from the sacred patrimony of truth received from the Fathers. But at the same time she must ever look to the present, to the new conditions and new forms of life introduced into the modern world which have opened new avenues to the Catholic apostolate.... The substance of the ancient doctrine of the deposit of faith is one thing, and the way in which it is presented is another" (*DV*, 714, 715). Truth transcends opinions and feelings. When one is open enough and knows how to discern the signs of the times, one should prayerfully allow the Holy Spirit to work at every level in the Church and human history as part of the divine plan. In this sense, and because of the new climate created by Pope John, the Fathers of the Council learned very quickly that they should take their own responsibilities and not be too much in awe of "Rome" — of the curia's decisions, as if they were infallible. With the Council, the assembled Fathers learned that they themselves, always under the pope, held the real power, and that the members of the curia were like themselves, good, dedicated, and well-intentioned people, but fallible too.

9. *Acknowledging the inevitability of opposing points of views.* While perceiving his office as a sign of unity and harmony and as an instrument for reconciliation and peace, Pope John was the first to recognize that opposing points of views are real and an inevitable part of the effort to reach the most adequate expression of faith. Indeed, "Everything, even human

differences," he said, "leads to the greater good of the Church" (*DV*, 713). He once dismissed the importance of disagreements at the Council by saying: "We're not friars singing in a choir." And to the French bishops with whom he met after the first session of the Council, he confided: "Yes, there's an argument going on. That's all right. It must happen. But it should be done in a fraternal spirit. It will all work out. *Moi, je suis optimiste*" (As for me, I am an optimist).[8] On another occasion he said: "Even among cultured and spiritual people there may be a variety of opinions and views in matters open to discussion. This does no harm to charity and peace, as long as we preserve moderation of manner and harmony of minds. I will add moreover that the Lord makes use of these misunderstandings to bring about in other ways some great good" (*PD*, 139).

10. *Living a holy optimism.* When one trusts in God and learns to discern God's voice, one cannot but be optimistic. When Pope John had the idea of calling a council, for example, he knew how enormous the difficulties could be. But he trusted God's plan and saw in the Council one of God's greatest graces to the Church and the world and an exceptional opportunity to expand the message of the Gospel. And he rejected categorically the opinions of "those prophets of gloom, who are always forecasting disaster, as though the end of the world were at hand" (*DV*, 712). Moreover, optimism seemed to have been in his very temperament and type of personality. Indeed, early on, at the age of twenty-one, "cheerfulness at all times" (*JS*, 96) was one of his aspirations. He wanted this for himself and he tried to encourage it in others. His attitude was basically and practically a rejection of the existentialist slogan of the twentieth century, "Others are hell," which was increasingly spreading at that time. For him, it was the path of joy and good communication with others that must prevail.

11. *Acknowledging the importance of openness and dialogue with those who are not Catholic.* In his encyclical *Ad Petri*

Cathedram, Pope John, citing St. Augustine, wrote: "We address, then, as brethren all who are separated from Us, using the words of Saint Augustine: 'Whether they wish or not, they are our brethren. They cease to be our brethren only when they stop saying 'Our Father'" (no. 86). He also wrote elsewhere: "The Church . . . does not identify itself with any one culture, not even with European and Western civilization, although the history of the Church is closely intertwined with it; for the mission entrusted to the Church pertains chiefly to other matters, that is, to matters which are concerned with religion and the eternal salvation of men" (Address to Writers and Artists, quoted in *PP,* 19). Pope John was ready to be open to anyone, even to non-Christians. It was reported that he once said about the Soviet leader Nikita Khrushchev: "If this fine gentleman came to Rome and asked to see me, why should I refuse? I would listen to him."[9]

12. *Striving toward a new order of human relations.* "In the present order of things," Pope John said in his opening speech to the Second Vatican Council, "Divine providence is leading us to a new order of human relations which, by men's own efforts and even beyond their very expectations, are directed toward the fulfillment of God's superior and inscrutable designs" (*DV,* 712–13). The pope made this theme of human relations an important part of his life and teaching. No wonder many recognized his "genius for human relationships" (*IT,* 60). His own deep humanity was widely recognized. Maurice Ragsdale, the editor of *Reader's Digest,* in asking Lawrence Elliott to write a book about this pope, said: "I think what we're after here is the story of a man. He happened to become pope, but people didn't love him because he was high and mighty but, just the opposite, because he was so human. And the human side of it — the whole business of his terrific appeal to non-Christians — is probably easier told from the outside looking in" (*CJ,* ix). A new order of human relations requires being very human first.

A good example of this would be what he said one time, recalling a meeting he must have had during his nunciature in Paris: "We did not debate, we talked; we did not discuss, but we became fond of each other!" (*JTP,* 260). Another good example is what he said in his farewell speech to the Bulgarian people in November 1934:

> According to a tradition still preserved in Catholic Ireland, on Christmas Eve every house sets a light in the window, in order to let Joseph and Mary know, in case they are passing by that night, looking for shelter, that inside there is a family, awaiting them around the fire and around the table laden with the gifts of God. Dear brothers, no one knows the ways of the future! Wherever I might go in the world, if someone from Bulgaria should pass by my house, at night, in distress, he will find a lamp lit in my window. Knock! Knock! I will not ask you if you are a Catholic or not; it is enough that you are my brother from Bulgaria: enter! Two brotherly arms will embrace you, the warm heart of a friend will welcome you. For such is the Christian charity of the Lord, expressions of which have sweetened my life during my ten years' sojourn in Bulgaria. (*JTP,* 168–69)

Pope John was a great master in the art of relating to others. People trusted him because they knew he wished them well, and they reciprocated this feeling. Although a man of great intelligence, he was, in a more particular way, a man guided first by his heart when it came to human relations.

13. *Attaining the common good.* Pope John, especially in his two encyclicals *Mater et Magistra* and *Pacem in Terris,* saw the connection that exists between the common good and human nature, and emphasized the necessity of choosing, promoting, and achieving this common good. He wrote, for example: "The common good, since it is intimately bound up with human nature, can never exist fully and completely unless the human

person is taken into account at all times. . . . Every civil authority must strive to promote the common good in the interest of all, without favoring any individual citizen or category of citizen. . . . There will always be an imperative need — born of man's very nature — to promote in sufficient measure the universal common good; the good, that is, of the whole human family" (*PT,* 55, 56, 132).

14. *Creating true peace.* Long before he was directly involved in the Cuban missile crisis in October 1962 and before he wrote his masterpiece on peace *Pacem in Terris,* Pope John had always linked peace to truth, justice, brotherhood, and the effort to live in harmony with the teachings of the Gospel. In his retreat of 1940, for example, he remarked: "War . . . is desired by men, deliberately, in defiance of the most sacred laws. That is what makes it so evil. He who instigates war and foments it is always the 'Prince of the world,' who has nothing to do with Christ, the 'Prince of Peace'" (John 12:31; 16:11) (*JS,* 239). Christians should never forget that Jesus is the Prince of Peace, and that working for peace is not an optional choice for them. Peace on all fronts — peace of heart, peace in families, peace between different groups, peace between nations — is a constitutive part of the Christian life. This is why every Christian and every person of good will should, in the footsteps of Pope John, consider peacemaking central to their faith and humanness.

15. *Full participation of the laity in the life of the Church.* One important part of Pope John's great legacy was certainly to allow the full participation of the laity in the Church. Throughout his encyclicals and in many other occasions, he reiterated his desire to see the engagement of Christians, pointing out to them the responsibility they have toward the expansion of God's kingdom. He would say for example: "The Christian faithful, members of a living organism, cannot remain aloof and think that they have done their duty when they have satisfied their own spiritual needs; every individual must give his

assistance to those who are working for the increase and propagation of God's kingdom" (*PP*, 40). So, gone the days of uneducated members of the Church who passively sit in the pews, ready just to "pray, pay, and obey." Gone that yesteryear definition of the laity as "neither priest nor monk." Gone the narrow structures of "clericalism," "legalism," and "triumphalism." Now, after Pope John and his Council, we rather talk about the "people of God," filled with the gifts of the Holy Spirit.

Pope John XXIII was the common man who happened to become a pope. It is a fact that he had neither the ingenious mind nor the majestic and *ex cathedra* attitude of his predecessor Pius XII, but it is also a fact that people were fascinated with his earthiness and simplicity, his humility and goodness, his heart-centeredness, and warmth. The drive of his charismatic personality, his palpable respect for others, and his readiness to open a dialogue and try new experiences shaped in him the inviting approach to life that he radiated. He was not anxious about anything, and he was distrustful of no one. He trusted divine providence. His rock-solid faith made him insist that, "we believe confidently that God is at work in the conscience of the individual person, that he is present in history" (*PSB*, 156). His decisions came as a result not of a conceptual system but from a life lived in accordance with the Gospel truth.

In many ways, Pope John can be considered a role model for everyone, especially for those in posts of authority — Church leaders as well as state leaders. He teaches us much about the style of life that Christ lived.

All in all, when Pope John appealed to people of good will, he did not use this appeal as a diplomatic tool to carry out a self-serving agenda. He did it sincerely, wholeheartedly, and resolutely because he believed in brotherhood and especially because he believed in the power of the Holy Spirit who is working in the world. With this, he proved to be farsighted indeed. While he refused to "depart from the sacred patrimony of truth received from the Fathers," he "[looked] ... to the new conditions and new forms of life introduced into the modern world" (*DV*, 714), and witnessed the opening of new horizons. And with humble words and the gestures of an old man who loved the past, he was able to pinpoint the guidelines of the future toward a "new Pentecost." His overflowing love and respect for everyone, his advocacy for peace, social justice, and reform, and his freshness of approach to ecclesiastical affairs made him one of the most loved and popular popes of all times.

From his unique position in place and time in the history of the Church and the world, Pope John, by allowing the Holy Spirit to work freely in and through him, was able to cast the rock of his weighty contribution in the ocean of human affairs, thus creating a ring of waves that is ceaselessly expanding, wider and wider, and further and further.

Notes

1. Robert Ellsberg, *All Saints: Daily Reflections on Saints, Prophets, and Witnesses for Our Time* (New York: Crossroad, 1997), 243.

2. Quoted in Thomas Cahill, *Pope John XXIII* (New York: Viking-Penguin Group, 2002), ix.

3. Ibid.

4. G. K. Chesterton, *Orthodoxy* (New York: John Lane Company, 1908), 212.

5. See *America*, October 28, 2002, 15–16.

6. Nancy Celaschi, O.S.F., "One of the Best-Loved Popes of the 20th Century Is Being Beatified This Month...," *St. Anthony Messenger* (September 2000): 33.

7. See *America*, February 10, 2003, 21.

8. See "Anniversary Thoughts: Ten Lessons from 'Good Pope John' " in *America*, October 7, 2002, 14.

9. Ibid., 13.

1

Called to Holiness

Throughout his life — as early as his youngest years to the last day of his pontificate — Pope John XXIII's deepest desire was to become a holy person. He expressed this desire on many occasions and took practical steps to achieve that goal. Along with profound examinations of conscience and weekly confession, he used traditional tools such as prayer, the liturgy, the breviary, and spiritual reading, especially, the lives of the saints. He also included meditation, visits to the Blessed Sacrament, the rosary, annual retreats, and works of mercy. But above all, with utmost humility, he came to know himself very well, and he knew that he had to trust God and surrender to the divine will. His total abandonment to divine providence freed him from the pressure of the unnecessary things in life and helped him to focus on what matters most: "Our blessed Jesus Christ, his holy Church, his Gospel, and in the Gospel above all else the Our Father according to the mind and heart of Jesus, and the truth and goodness of his Gospel" (JS, 344). No wonder, then, Pope John had to have a "holy optimism" and a good and refined sense of humor that translated his intense love for God, for life, for family, and for all his fellow human beings.

THE PURSUIT OF HOLINESS

I renew my resolution to make myself really holy, and I protest once more before you, O most loving Heart of Jesus, my Teacher, that I wish to love you as you desire, and to be filled with your spirit. Meanwhile, there are four resolutions which I am determined to carry out here, now and always, so as to be able to take a few steps forward. First of all I must have the spirit of union with Jesus, the spirit of recollection in his Heart from my first awakening in the morning until I close my eyes at night and, if possible, also during my dreams at night. "I slept but my heart was awake" (Song of Solomon 5:2). My best efforts must go into saying the rosary. Secondly, I must never forget the dictum: *Age quod agis!* ("Pay attention to what you are doing") and always and in all my actions preserve presence of mind. Thirdly, I must observe the most scrupulous modesty in my glances, words, etc. We know what we mean by this. Finally, tranquility, calm, cheerfulness, good manners, never a cross word with anyone, no excited speech, but simplicity, cordiality, sincerity without cowardice — no flabbiness. And I must add: never to speak of anyone, or of my intimate friends, if their failures should set my own conduct in a better light. If I speak at all I must speak with reserve, saying what good I can of them and covering up their failings when to reveal them would do no good and would only arouse my own vanity which lurks beneath the surface and more often than not quietly slips out. These are the fruits of this retreat.

O Jesus, you see the deep desire of my heart to love you, to become a real minister of yours; grant me the grace really to do a little good. Shall I be able to carry out these modest resolutions? O Jesus, I hope so much from your grace. (*Recollection of August 22, 1900*)   —*JS*, 75

Today was a perfect feast; I spent it in the company of St. Francis de Sales, my gentlest of saints. What a magnificent figure of a man, priest, and bishop! If I were like him, I would not mind even if they were to make me pope! I love to let my thoughts dwell on him, on his goodness and on his teaching. I have read his life so many times! His counsels are so acceptable to my heart. By the light of his example I feel more inclined toward humility, gentleness and calm. My life, so the Lord tells me, must be a perfect copy of that of St. Francis de Sales if I wish it to bear good fruits. Nothing extraordinary in me or in my behavior, except my way of doing ordinary things: "all ordinary things but done in no ordinary way." A great, a burning love for Jesus Christ and his Church: unalterable serenity of mind, wonderful gentleness with my fellow men, that is all.

O my loving saint, as I kneel before you at this moment, there is so much I could say to you! I love you tenderly and I will always remember you and look to you for help. O St. Francis, I can say no more; you can see into my heart; give me what I need to become like you. (*Spiritual notes*, January 29, 1903)
— *JS*, 110

My obligation to aim at sanctification at all costs must be ever present in my mind, but it must be a serene and tranquil preoccupation, not wearisome and overmastering. I must remember it at every moment, from when I first open my eyes to the morning light till I close them in sleep at night. So, no slipping back into old ways and customs. Serenity and peace, but perseverance and determination. A total distrust and poor opinion of myself, accompanied by uninterrupted and loving union with God. This is my task, this my labor. O good Jesus, help me. "Mary, show that you are my Mother." (*Spiritual notes*, February 2, 1903)
— *JS*, 111

What has Mgr. Roncalli been doing during these monotonous years at the Apostolic Delegation? Trying to make himself holy and with simplicity, kindness, and joy opening a source of blessings and graces for all Bulgaria, whether he lives to see it or not.

This is what ought to be. But these are grand words and still grander things. O my Jesus, it shames me to think of them; I blush to speak of them. But give me the grace, the power, the glory of making this come true. The rest does not matter. All the rest is vanity, worthlessness, and affliction of the soul.

Jesus, Mary, Joseph, my heart and soul are yours, now and forever. (*Retreat of August 27–31, 1934*)   —*JS*, 223

My only wish is that my life should end in a holy manner. I tremble at the thought of having to bear pain, responsibilities, or difficulties beyond my poor capacity, but I trust in the Lord, without claiming any successes or extraordinary or brilliant merit. (*Retreat of April 10–12, 1952*)   —*JS*, 280

I am beginning my direct ministry at an age — seventy-two years — when others end theirs. So, *I find myself on the threshold of eternity.* O Jesus, chief Shepherd and Bishop of our souls, the mystery of my life and death is in your hands, close to your heart. On the one hand I tremble at the approach of my last hour; on the other hand I trust in you and only look one day ahead. I feel I am in the same condition as St. Aloysius Gonzaga, that is, I must go on with what I have to do, always striving after perfection but thinking still more of God's mercy.

In the few years I have still to live, *I want to be a holy pastor,* in the full sense of the word, like the Blessed Pius X, my predecessor, and the revered Cardinal Ferrari, and my own Mgr. Radini Tedeschi while he lived, and as he would have remained had he lived longer. "So help me God." (*Retreat of May 15–21, 1953*)   —*JS*, 283

In the last month, since October 28, when my name and official title were changed, I've had this experience: I hear people

talking about the pope, in indirect or direct speech. For example, "The pope should be told this" or "This will have to be
dealt with by the pope." When I hear this I still think of the
Holy Father Pope Pius XII, whom I venerated and loved so
much, forgetting that the person they are talking about is *me,*
who chose to be called John.

Very slowly I'm getting used to the new forms of speech involved in my new ministry. Yes, I am, most unworthily, "the
servant of the servants of God," because the Lord willed it; the
Lord, not I. But every time I hear someone address me as "Your
Holiness," you can't imagine how embarrassed and thoughtful
it makes me.

Ah! My sons — *saltem vos amici mei* (at least you are my
friends) — ask the Lord in prayer that I may be granted the
grace of the holiness that is attributed to me. For it is one thing
to say it or believe it, and quite another to be holy. The grace of
the Lord can raise you much higher than his humble and faithful servant; but nothing counts, nothing has value for history
and human life, nothing has any value for the Church and for
souls, unless the pontiff is holy in deed as well as in title.

My sons, pray for me to the Madonna, Mother of Jesus and
our dearest Mother, pray to the two famous Johns whose cult
flourishes in St. John Lateran nearby.... This is what I wanted
to say to you. It comes sincerely from the heart and is a great
consolation for me, and for all of us it is an encouragement and
a joy. — *PJS,* 301–2

I must always hold myself ready to die, even a sudden death,
and also to live as long as it pleases the Lord to leave me here
below. Yes, always. At the beginning of my eightieth year I
must hold myself ready: for death or life, for the one as for
the other, and I must see to the saving of my soul. Everyone
calls me "Holy Father," and holy I must and will be. (*Retreat
of August 10–15, 1961*) — *JS,* 303

Considering the purpose of my own life I must:

1. Desire only to be virtuous and holy, and so be pleasing to God.

2. Direct all things, thoughts as well as actions, to the increase, the service, and the glory of Holy Church.

3. Recognize that I have been set here by God, and therefore remain perfectly serene about all that happens, not only as regards myself but also with regard to the Church, continuing to work and suffer with Christ, for her good.

4. Entrust myself at all times to divine providence.

5. Always acknowledge my own nothingness.

6. Always arrange my day in an intelligent and orderly manner. (*Retreat of August 10–15, 1961*)   —*JS*, 311

What Is a Saint?

Practical experience has now convinced me of this: the concept of holiness which I had formed and applied to myself was mistaken. In every one of my actions, and in the little failings of which I was immediately aware, I used to call to mind the image of some saint whom I had set myself to imitate down to the smallest particular, as a painter makes an exact copy of a picture by Raphael. I used to say to myself: in this case St. Aloysius would have done so and so, or: he would not do this or that. However, it turned out that I was never able to achieve what I had thought I could do, and this worried me. The method was wrong. From the saints I must take the substance, not the accidents, of their virtues. I am not St. Aloysius, nor must I seek holiness in his particular way, but according to the requirements of my own nature, my own character, and the different conditions of my life. I must not be the dry, bloodless reproduction of a model, however perfect. God desires us to follow the examples of the saints by absorbing the vital sap of their virtues and turning it into our own life-blood, adapting it to our own individual capacities and particular circumstances. If St. Aloysius had been as I am, he would have become holy in a different way. (*Spiritual notes, January 16, 1903*)   —*JS*, 106–17

The Gospel: Fullness of Holiness

The Gospel contains the fullness of holiness. It presents it to us in the most attractive light, gently tempered to our frail sight. In these pages we contemplate in fact the Man God, who is supreme, infinite perfection. To the pure and beautiful light already seen in the Old Testament saints, the Gospel now adds the most daring counsels, which raise virtue to the heights of heroism. It preaches worship in spirit and in truth, set free from the old observance, the old Law grown sterile; it preaches the love, rather than the fear, of God, the trustful love of a son for his father rather than the servant's trembling respect for his master. It teaches us to be "poor in spirit," to feel indifferent to wealth, to strip ourselves of possessions we might legitimately keep without ceasing to be good; it means giving our wealth to the poor.

It means simplicity, purity of heart, and humility, even welcoming insults and rejoicing in suffering, forgiving offences, showing charity to our enemies, with forgetfulness of self and self-denial. It may even mean dying for those we love. In short, it is all that is most directly opposed to the faulty inclinations of our nature, all that most resembles and most nearly approaches the divine perfection. This is the Gospel; and besides giving us the fullness of sublimity and holiness it shows us also the continuation and harmonious fulfillment of the historical themes of the Old Testament.   —*PD*, 212

What does the world know of that mysterious force which stirs in the depths of so many souls who seem unsatisfied in this world because they follow another light, an ideal which never fails to attract them?

In recent times, because of a fashion that seems to me a legitimate reaction to certain traditional methods of recounting the lives of holy men (methods according to which the saints were plucked by the hair and dragged out of the society in which they lived, and even out of themselves, to be turned into demigods), we have, perhaps a little too eagerly, turned to the opposite excess and concentrated too much on the study of the human element in the saint, and by so doing have to some extent failed to give enough consideration to the work of grace.

What is a saint? Recent distortions have tended to spoil our conception of the saints; they have been tricked out and colored with certain garish tints, which might perhaps be tolerated in a novel but which are out of place in the real world and in practical life.

To deny oneself at all times, to suppress, within oneself and in external show, all that the world would deem worthy of praise, to guard in one's own heart the flame of most pure love for God, far surpassing the frail affections of this world, to give all and sacrifice all for the good of others, and with humility and trust, in the love of God and of one's fellow men, to obey the laws laid down by providence, and follow the way which leads chosen souls to the fulfillment of their mission — and everyone has his mission — this is holiness, and all holiness is but this.   — *PD*, 44–45

"KNOW THYSELF"

Man is never so great as when he is on his knees. This is a fine saying, worthy of that great champion of Christ, Louis Veuillot. I must bear it well in mind, and always. Therefore it is not learning that is really the height of greatness and glory, but knowledge of ourselves, of our nothingness before God and of our need of God, without which we are but puny creatures, although we raise ourselves up to the stature of giants, O Mary! (*Spiritual notes, February 18, 1903*) — *JS*, 112–13

I wish to speak to you with the utmost frankness of heart and speech.

You have eagerly awaited me; things have been written and said about me which far surpass my deserts. Now I humbly introduce myself.

Like every other man who lives on this earth, I come from a family and from a clearly defined starting point: with the grace of good bodily health, with enough common sense to enable me to understand things quickly and clearly, with a loving disposition toward men which keeps me faithful to the teaching of the Gospel, respectful of my own rights as of those of others, and incapable of doing ill to anyone; indeed it encourages me to do good to all.

I am of humble birth and I was trained to a contented and blessed poverty, which makes few demands and fosters the growth of the most noble and lofty virtues, a good preparation for the higher altitude of life.

Providence took me from my native village and made me travel along the roads of this world in the East and in the West, bringing me into touch with people of different religions and ideologies, at grips with social problems which are acute and menacing, and meanwhile preserved my serenity, a balanced judgment, and a spirit of enquiry. I was always engaged, naturally, with fidelity to the principles of Catholic belief and moral teaching, more with what unites men than with what divides them and provokes conflicts. . . .

These notes give you the modest physiognomy of the man before you.

Certainly, the position that has been entrusted to me in Venice is a great one, and far in excess of my deserts. But above all I wish to commend to your benevolence the man who wishes simply to be your brother, friendly, approachable and understanding. I intend to follow the same course which has served me well till now, and which has perhaps brought about my return to Venice, to live among a noble people particularly sensitive to the impulses of the heart, to simplicity of behavior, of speech, of works, to that respectful and cheerful sincerity of dealings which is characteristic, even if within limited proportions, of the man who has deserved the title of a man of proven honesty, of an honest man without a stain who is worthy of confident respect.

This is the man, this is the new citizen whom Venice has today been pleased to welcome with such festive rejoicings.

— *JTP*, 84–86

My poor life, now such a long one, has unwound itself as easily as a ball of string, under the sign of simplicity and purity. It costs me nothing to acknowledge and repeat that *I am nothing and worth precisely nothing.*

The Lord caused me to be born of poor folk, and he has seen to all my needs. I have left it to him. As a young priest I was struck by the motto *Oboedientia et Pax* of Cesare Baronius, who used to say it as he bowed his head to kiss the foot of St. Peter's statue — and I have left everything to God and have allowed myself to be led in perfect obedience to the plans of providence. Truly, "the will of God is my peace." And my hope is all in the mercy of God, who wanted me to be his priest and minister. He has been too kind about my "countless sins, offences and negligences" (Roman Missal, Offertory prayer) and he still keeps me full of life and vigor. (*Retreat of June 2–7, 1957*)

— *JS*, 291–92

"I Keep True to My Principle"

My present: here I am then, still alive, in my sixty-ninth year, prostrate over the crucifix, kissing the face of Christ and his sacred wounds, kissing his heart, laid bare in his pierced side; here I am showing my love and grief. How could I not feel grateful to Jesus, finding myself still young and robust of body, spirit, and heart? "Know thyself": this keeps me humble and without pretensions. Some people feel admiration and affection for my humble person; but thanks be to God, I still blush for myself, my insufficiencies, and my unworthiness in this important position where the Holy Father has placed me, and still keeps me, out of the kindness of his heart. For some time past I have cultivated simplicity, which comes very easily to me, cheerfully defying all those clever people who, looking for the qualities required in a diplomat of the Holy See, prefer the outer covering to the sound ripe fruit beneath. And I keep true to my principle which seems to me to have a place of honor in the Sermon on the Mount: blessed are the poor, the meek, the peacemakers, the merciful, those who hunger and thirst for righteousness, the pure in heart, the suffering and the persecuted (see Matt. 5:3–10). My present, then, is spent in faithful service to Christ, who was obedient and was crucified, words I repeat so often at this season: "Christ was made obedient" (see Phil. 2:8). So I must be meek and humble like him, glowing with divine charity, ready for sacrifice or for death, for him or for his Church. (*Retreat of April 6–7, 1959*)   —*JS*, 275–76

The welcome immediately accorded to my unworthy person and the affection still shown by all who approach me are always a source of surprise to me. The maxim "Know thyself" suffices for my spiritual serenity and keeps me on the alert. The secret of my success must lie there: in not "searching into things which are above my ability" (Ecclus. 3:22) and in being content to be "meek and humble of heart." Meekness and humbleness of heart give graciousness in receiving, speaking, and dealing with people, and the patience to bear, to pity, to keep silent, and to encourage. Above all, one must always be ready for the Lord's surprise moves, for although he treats his loved ones well, he generally likes to test them with all sorts of trials such as bodily infirmities, bitterness of soul, and sometimes opposition so powerful as to transform and wear out the life of the servant of God, the life of the servant of the servants of God, making it a real martyrdom. I always think of Pius IX of sacred and glorious memory and, by imitating him in his sufferings, I would like to be worthy to celebrate his canonization. (*Retreat of November 29–December 5, 1959*)   —*JS*, 299

My failings and incapacities, and my "countless sins, offences, and negligences" for which I offer my daily Mass, are a cause of constant interior mortification, which prevents me from indulging in any kind of self-glorifications but does not weaken my confidence and trust in God, whose caressing hand I feel upon me, sustaining and encouraging.

Nor do I ever feel tempted to vanity or complacency. "What little I know about myself is enough to make me feel ashamed." What a fine saying that is, which Manzoni put in the mouth of Cardinal Federico!

"In thee, O God, have I hoped; let me never be confounded" (Ps. 30 [31]:2)

At the beginning of my eightieth year it is all-important for me to humble myself and lose myself in the Lord, trusting that in his mercy he will open for me the gate to eternal life. Jesus, Mary, Joseph, may I breathe forth my soul in peace with you! (*Retreat of November 27–December 3, 1960*)   —*JS*, 301

As my retreat draws to an end, I see very clearly the substance of the task which Jesus in his providence has allowed to be entrusted to me.

"Vicar of Christ?" Ah, I am not worthy of this name, I, the humble child of Battista and Marianna Roncalli, two good

Christians to be sure, but so modest and humble! Yet that is what I must be; the vicar of Christ. "Priest and victim"; the priesthood fills me with joy, but the sacrifice implied in the priesthood makes me tremble.

Blessed Jesus, God and man! I renew the consecration of myself to you, for life, for death, for eternity. (*Retreat of August 10–15, 1961*) —*JS, 315*

On this kinship is based the mission and office of the chief pontiff of the Holy Catholic Church, the "vicar of Christ," as I am called. Oh how profoundly I feel the meaning and the emotion of the "Lord I am not worthy" which I say every morning, in token of humility and love, when I take the sacred host in my hands. (*Retreat of November 26–December 2, 1961*) —*JS, 320*

SURRENDER TO GOD'S WILL

It is my studies that are most on my mind during these days. All this really boils down to a question of pride. We think we cannot be really great men unless we are supremely learned. But this is to use the same standards as the world, and we must get used to taking a different view. My real greatness lies in doing the will of God, entirely and perfectly. If God required me to burn my books or to become a poor lay brother, set to do the most humiliating tasks in some out-of-the-way and despised monastery, my heart would bleed, but I should have to do it, and in so doing I should become really great. So for goodness' sake let us not get too agitated about it. "Not too much of anything." (*Spiritual notes, February 6, 1903*) —*JS, 111–12*

The fundamental principles of the spiritual life still hold firm, thanks be to God: to feel wholly detached from my own nothingness and to remind myself that, in the words of the Ambrosian Mass, I am the least of all, and a sinner. I must abandon myself completely to the will of the Lord and desire to live for nothing else but the apostolate and the faithful service of Holy Church. I must feel no concern about my future and be ready to sacrifice everything, even life itself — should the Lord think me worthy — for the glory of God and the accomplishment of my duty; I must have a great spiritual fervor, in keeping with the mind of the Church and the best tradition, without any exaggeration of external forms or methods, but constant zeal and mildness, with an eye for everything, always with great patience and gentleness, remembering what Cardinal Mercier quotes from Gratry: Gentleness is the fullness of strength. And finally, I must always be familiar with the thought of death, which helps so much to make life carefree and joyful. (*Retreat of October 25–31, 1942*)

—*JS*, 259

Old age, likewise a great gift of the Lord's, must be for me a source of *tranquil inner joy* and a reason for trusting day by day in the Lord himself, to whom I am now turned as a child turns to his father's open arms. (*Retreat of June 2–7, 1957*)

—*JS*, 291

"Jesus Christ, yesterday and today and the same for ever" (Heb. 13:8).

Not to try to predict the future, indeed not to count on any future at all: that is my rule of conduct, inspired by that spirit of tranquility and constancy from which the faithful and my collaborators must receive light and encouragement from the pope, the head priest.

The source of priesthood is Christ, as St. Thomas assures us (*S.T.*, III, q.22, ad.4): "The priest of the Old Testament was a figure of Christ, the priest of the new law functions in the person of Christ himself." This must be said in the first place of the pope, both because of the pope's conscience, which is felt to be invested with the presence, the grace, and the light of Christ, and because of the fact that he entrusts everything to Christ, all the thoughts and operations of his many-sided apostolic activity. It is enough to take thought for the present: it is not necessary to be curious and anxious about the shape of things to come. The vicar of Christ knows what Christ wants from him and does not have to come before him to offer him advice or to insist on his plans. The pope's basic rule of conduct must be always to content himself with his present state and have no concern for the future; this he must accept from the Lord as it comes, but without counting on it or making any human provision for it, even taking care not to speak of it confidently and casually to anyone.

My experience during these three years as pope, since "in fear and trembling" I accepted this service in pure obedience to the Lord's will, conveyed to me through the voice of the Sacred College of Cardinals in conclave, bears witness to this maxim and is a moving and lasting reason for me to be true to it: absolute trust in God, in all that concerns the present, and perfect tranquility as regards the future.

The various initiatives of a pastoral character which mark this first stage of my papal apostolate have all come to me as pure, tranquil, loving, I might even say silent, inspirations from the Lord, speaking to the heart of his poor servant who, through no merit of his own save that very simple merit of mere acquiescence and obedience, without discussion, has been able to contribute to the honor of Jesus and the edification of souls. (*Retreat of August 10–15, 1961*)   —*JS*, 313–14

In the eyes of the Lord I am a sinner and nothing but dust: I live by the mercy of Jesus, to whom I owe everything and from whom I expect everything. I submit to him even if he wishes me to be wholly transformed by his pains and his sufferings, in the entire abandonment of absolute obedience and conformity with his will. Now more than ever, and as long as I live, and in all things, *oboedientia et pax*. (*Retreat of August 10–15, 1961*)

—*JS*, 307

HOLINESS AND
THE PRACTICE OF VIRTUES

Detachment

From the transient things of this world the mind soars to the grandeur of heaven; from the vain glitter of worldly pomp to the serene splendor of virtue. It is so consoling to think of today's saint who, lowly and despised, was found worthy to do the most energetic and important work for the good of the Church. "God chose what is weak in the world to shame the strong" (see 1 Cor. 1:27–28), and we see this perfectly exemplified in the great virgin saint of Siena, St. Catherine.

She who thought only of humbling herself and living in seclusion, loving her divine Spouse, was chosen to restore peace to the Church by recalling the pope to Rome. In comparison with her, what are the wise men, the conquerors, the great ones of her age? What a sublime lesson for my pride and at the same time what a reason for confidence in God to whom all things are possible, who makes up for our failings and teaches us to be really great, in his own eyes and in the eyes of the world. (*Spiritual notes, April 30, 1903*)　　　　　　　　　　　　　　　—*JS*, 123

There is no lack of rumor around me, murmurs that "greater things are in store." I am not so foolish as to listen to this flattery, which is, yes, I admit it, for me too a temptation. I try very hard to ignore these rumors, which speak of deceit and spite. I treat them as a joke: I smile and pass on. For the little, or nothing, that I am worth to the Holy Church, I have already my purple mantle, my blushes of shame at finding myself in this position of honor and responsibility when I know I am worth so little. Oh what a comfort it is to me to feel free from these longings for changes and promotions! I consider this freedom a great gift of God. May the Lord preserve me always in this state of mind. (*Retreat of November 12–18, 1939*)　　　　　　　—*JS*, 232

This year providence has placed considerable sums of money in my hands for my own personal use. I have distributed it all, some to the poor, some for my own needs and the needs of members of my family, and the rest, the main part, for the restoration of the Apostolic Delegation and some of my priests' rooms at the Holy Spirit. According to this world's judgments, which can penetrate even the sacred inner recesses of clerical life, and according to the criteria of human prudence, I have been a fool.

In fact, now I am poor again. Blessed be the Lord. I think that, by his grace, I did the right thing. Again I trust in his generosity for the future. "Give and it shall be given unto you" (Luke 6:38). (*Retreat of November 25–December 1, 1940*) —*JS, 237*

Born poor, but of humble and respected folk, I am particularly happy to die poor, having distributed, according to the various needs and circumstances of my simple and modest life in the service of the poor and of the holy Church which has nurtured me, whatever came into my hands — and it was very little — during the years of my priesthood and episcopate. Appearances of wealth have frequently disguised thorns of frustrating poverty which prevented me from giving to others as generously as I would have wished. I thank God for this grace of poverty to which I vowed fidelity in my youth, poverty of spirit, as a priest of the Sacred Heart, and material poverty, which has strengthened me in my resolve never to ask for anything — positions, money, or favors — never, either for myself or for my relations and friends. (*Spiritual testament and final dispositions of June 29, 1954*) —*JS, 343*

Kindness

I will be more and more careful to rule my tongue. I must be more guarded in the expression of my opinions, even with persons of my own household. This must once more become the object of the particular examinations of conscience. Nothing must escape my lips other than praise or the most mildly expressed disapproval or general exhortations to charity, to the apostolate, to virtuous living.

It is my nature to talk too much. A ready tongue is one of God's good gifts but it must be handled with care and respect, that is, with moderation, so that I may be welcome and not found a bore.

In my dealings with all, Catholics and Orthodox, high and low, I must always endeavor to leave an impression of dignity and loving-kindness, a radiant kindness and a pleasing dignity. To these people I represent, however unworthily, the Holy Father. It must therefore be my aim to make him loved and esteemed, even in my own person. This is what the Lord desires. What a task! What a responsibility! (*Retreat of November 9–13, 1927*)
— *JS*, 210–11

My own temperament inclines me toward compliance and a readiness to appreciate the good side of people and things, rather than to criticize and pronounce harsh judgments. This and the considerable difference in age, mine being more full of experience and profound understanding of the human heart, often make me feel painfully out of sympathy with my entourage. Any kind of distrust or discourtesy shown to anyone, especially to the humble, poor, or socially inferior, every destructive or thoughtless criticism, makes me writhe with pain. I say nothing, but my heart bleeds. These colleagues of mine are good ecclesiastics; I appreciate their excellent qualities, I am very fond of them and they deserve all my affection. And yet they cause me a lot of suffering. On certain days and in certain circumstances I am tempted to react violently. But I prefer to keep silence, trusting that this will be a more eloquent and effective lesson. Could this be weakness on my part? I must, I will continue to bear this light cross serenely, together with the mortifying sense of my own worthlessness, and I will leave everything else to God, who sees into all hearts and shows them the refinements of his love. (*Retreat of November 23–27, 1948*)
— *JS*, 271

Humility

I have a great need of recollection and concentration, and of reminding myself very often of the resolutions I make from time to time. Also, in everything I do, I must behave like a boy, the boy I really am, and not try to pass myself off as a serious philosopher and a man of importance. It is my natural inclination to do that — this is what I am made of: pride! For the rest, I must in all things resign myself to the will of God, bearing with patience and without irritability the misfortune God sends me in my own family, such as the serious illness of my little brother Giovanni [Giovanni was then seven years old].

Let us pray, let us pray always about everything, and may all be done according to the will of God, to his honor and glory.

Yes, "to the greater glory of God!" Amen. (*Spiritual notes, September 20, 1898*) —*JS, 45*

Last year in May I asked Mary for two things: humility and love. By the end of the month my prayer has been granted, for I had had occasion to practice both. This year I am back at the same point again, and I hope Our Lady will hear me again. She is so kind! To tell the truth, I find it hard to humble myself, but I hope this is an effort for which I shall be rewarded. It all depends on making a good start. Jesus, Mary, you know that I want to please you and to love you. (*Spiritual notes, May 7, 1899*) —*JS, 62*

The fact is that the more I speak about myself the more virtue I lose; vanity squirts out from every word, even from those which seem most innocent. I must get it into my head that when I am with others, my fellows or my Superiors, the best thing I can do is to preserve a becoming silence, or say only what is necessary or opportune; at least, never to speak about myself unless I am interrogated, and even then to say little and not try to hold my listener's attention. I must always consider that, because of my faults, I am unworthy to be with my companions. If I think this, how can I have the courage to sing my own praises before them? (*Spiritual diary of December 26, 1902*)   —*JS*, 100–101

My guiding principles remain the same: humility in everything, especially in my speech, union with God (the most important thing, of which I feel an even greater need today) and the will of God, and not my own, in all I do. I must mind my own business, think of myself and the pursuit of the devout life, without undue agitation. Intense, tranquil, and recollected study now; at all times and in all things great peace and sweetness in my heart. (*Spiritual notes, January 1, 1903*)   —*JS*, 103

At the beginning of my eightieth year it is all-important for me to humble myself and lose myself in the Lord, trusting that in his mercy he will open for me the gate to eternal life. Jesus, Mary, Joseph, may I breathe forth my soul in peace with you! (*Retreat of November 27–December 3, 1960*)   —*JS*, 301

Examination of Conscience

A month has already gone by since I came out from the holy Exercises. Where have I got to now in the way of virtue? Oh poor me!

Having made a general examination of my behavior during these recent days, I have found good reason to blush and feel humble. I have found that all my actions are far from perfect; I have not meditated satisfactorily; I have not heard Holy Mass in the way I should, because I have allowed myself to be distracted as soon as I got up, while I was washing myself; I have not paid my visit to the Blessed Sacrament with all the fervor I used to feel; I have made my general self-examination with very little, if any, profit; I have let my thoughts wander, especially during Vespers; I have given way to the languor that the hot weather brings. In a word, I find that I am still at the very beginning of the journey which I have undertaken, and this makes me feel ashamed. I thought I could have been a saint by this time, and instead I am still as miserable as before.

All this must humiliate me profoundly and make me realize what a good-for-nothing I am. Humility, humility, still more humility! However, in all my distress I can still thank the Lord for not having abandoned me as I deserved. Thanks be to God, I still have the will to be good, and with this I must go on. Go on, do I say? I must start again from the beginning. Well, I will do so. What am I waiting for? "In the name of the Father and of the Son and of the Holy Ghost, under the protection of the Virgin Mary and blessed Joseph" let us go forward.

These points, about which I must be more watchful, will help me to avoid the faults I have already mentioned. Enough! In the next retreat we shall see what stage we have got to! Meanwhile, God bless me. (*Spiritual notes, March 20, 1898*)   —*JS*, 19–20

I think this week has not been too bad. However, I must still reproach myself for not having been sufficiently attentive in class in certain periods, the literature lessons, and also for having sometimes yielded to the desire to play the wit, letting some foolish or frivolous expressions escape me. I have let my thoughts wander in the rosary, been full of distractions during my general examination of conscience, and rather inattentive also in my meditation. Alas! I have slipped back to where I was before. So I must try once more, with more enthusiasm, more attention, more humility. One of my failings is that I am never orderly, not even in spiritual matters, and yet I am always recommending orderliness to others.

I really must make sure that I never tell others to do what I do not try to practice myself, because until now I have been doing just the contrary. For example, those to whom I speak of love for Jesus in the Blessed Sacrament may perhaps get a very good impression of me in this respect, because I think I speak of this with the greatest fervor. But the truth is that I know I am still a

thousand miles behind, certainly a long way behind all my companions. I must put myself in order. Therefore, when I examine
my conscience I will concentrate on one particular fault and pay
the greatest attention to it. Now this week I will be particularly
attentive in the literature lessons and especially recollected in my
meditation, rosary, and general examination of conscience. For
the rest, humility always and in all things, especially with others,
never speaking of myself in the study circles, nor will I expose
the faults of others or encourage others to expose them, instead
of covering them up. (*Spiritual notes, June 12, 1898*)

—*JS*, 24–25

The other evening I had no candle, last night I had no ink, and
so for two evenings running I have written nothing.

When I look back over the last few days I must admit that even
if I cannot find any serious faults to deplore, I cannot find any
virtues either. I am still stuck in the same place, without moving
a step forward. I think all this is due to my not thinking about
it enough, not comparing one day with another and noting the
difference, as my particular examination of conscience requires,
which examination, by the way, I ought to make much more
carefully. In a word, there are some trifles which never seem to
come right or, to put it better, are never done really well: the
rosary, to some extent the visit also, and, much worse, the use
of invocations.

And yet I am not lacking in good intentions; for this I can only
thank the Lord, for it is all by his grace alone. But I must remind
myself that hell is full of good intentions. Oh, if I only knew how
necessary it is for me to be good and holy! Well, no more of this!
Tomorrow I am going to confession, and then I will begin a life
of greater application and fervor in honor of the Blessed Virgin,
who so greatly deserves my love. I will make a start by never
speaking with anyone, even in confidence, of small failings in
others, which perhaps I alone can see. O Mary! (*Spiritual notes,
August 12, 1898*)   —*JS*, 35–36

HOLINESS AND FAMILY

This is what I most desire for you, for I have never wished or implored from heaven for my family the good things of this world — wealth, pleasures, success — but rather that you should all be good Christians, virtuous and resigned in the loving arms of divine providence, and living at peace with everyone.

In fact what use would it be for us to possess even all the gold in the world at the price of losing our souls? Keep this truth firmly fixed in your minds and never forget it....

The Lord wants me to be a priest: that is why he has lavished so may gifts upon me, even sending me here to Rome, to be near his vicar, the pope, in the Holy City, near the tombs of so many illustrious martyrs and so many holy priests. This is a great good fortune for me and for you, for which you must always thank the good God.

But I am not going to be a priest just to please someone else, or to make money, or to find comfort, honors, or pleasures. God forbid! It is simply because I want to be able later on to be of some service to poor people, in whatever way I can. And that is why I would like you to be the first to benefit from this, you who have done so much for me, you whose spiritual welfare is so dear to my heart and for whom I pray every day, I might say every hour.

Will you give me the great joy of knowing that you have all received great good from the holy Mission, and that you have become better Christians than before? I hope this is so, indeed I am quite sure of it, knowing so well your excellent intentions.

Please remember me, all of you, at the general communion. Meanwhile accept my wishes and my greetings, and share these with all our relations and friends. (*Letter to his parents, Rome, January 16, 1901*)   —*JS, 329, 330*

Excessive attachment to members of one's own family which, when they are felt beyond the limits of charity, become an embarrassment and a hindrance. The law of the apostolate and the priesthood is above the law of flesh and blood. Therefore I must love my own kith and kin, and go to their assistance when their poverty makes this necessary, because this is an obvious duty for one who does so much to help strangers, but all must be done discreetly, in a purely priestly spirit, in an orderly and impartial manner. My closest relations, brothers, sisters, nephews, and nieces, with very few exceptions, are exemplary Christians and give me great joy. But it would never do for me to get mixed up in their affairs and concerns, so as to be diverted from my duties as a servant of the Holy See, and a bishop! (*Retreat of November 25–December 1, 1940*)   —*JS*, 251

My dear sisters, brothers, nephews, nieces, and relations,

As you see, some news spreads so quickly that the people it most concerns have no time to impart it themselves. So it is true: my humble name is included among the twenty-four churchmen whom the Holy Father, on January 12, will nominate cardinals of Holy Church. I am sure that you will be pleased to hear this: I too am pleased, more for your sakes than for my own.

Take everything simply and humbly, as I do. Even becoming a cardinal counts for nothing unless it leads to eternal salvation and sanctification. The Holy Father Pius X, now beatified, trod this same road, as did Cardinal Ferrari, who will also perhaps be beatified soon. To follow in their footsteps means a great deal to me; the rest, that is, the purple, the human honors, and the earthly satisfactions count for nothing at all.

I admit that this nomination gives me great joy when I think of you, humble Christian people as you are, and of our little native village, and of all who bear our name and are our kith and kin. In these times to have a cardinal in the family does not indicate wealth. I foresee that my material condition will be as before. I shall not lack what I need, but my family will still be living modestly. I too shall always be poor, but poor with honor and dignity. We shall speak of this again. Meanwhile, thank the Lord with me and ask him to make me a good cardinal, a peace-loving and gentle cardinal, working only for Holy Church and the souls of men. And do not worry about anything.

How glad I am that you, my dear brothers, were able to visit me in France last August! I cannot tell you now where providence, or better, the Holy Father speaking in the Lord's name, will wish me to work during these years to come, which will be the last years of life for me, and for us older folk. I am not trying to find a house in Rome or anywhere else. Everything will be made clear in the coming months, and I can assure you that all will be to my satisfaction and yours....

I beg you all to maintain absolute reserve about this and to behave with your usual simplicity. Beware especially of journalists: the best are indiscreet, even if their intentions are good. They already know quite enough about me, without your adding anything more.

I do not yet know even the circumstances of my receiving the cardinal's title, whether I shall have to go to Rome on January 12, to receive the biretta from the pope's hands, or whether it will be sent to me here so that the president of the republic may confer it. I will let you know as soon as I hear anything.

Meanwhile be calm, good, and very chary of words with people outside the family. I bless you all together. (November 30, 1952)

Your loving
+*Ang. Gius. Archbishop*
— *LHF,* 717–18

To my beloved family according to the flesh, from whom moreover I have never received any material wealth, I can leave only a great and special blessing, begging them to preserve that fear of God which made them always so dear and beloved to me, and to be simple and modest without ever being ashamed of it: it is their true title of nobility. I have sometimes come to their aid, as a poor man to the poor, but without lifting them out of their respected and contented poverty. I pray and I will ever pray for their welfare, glad as I am to see in their new and vigorous shoots the constancy and faithfulness to the religious tradition of the parent stock which will always be their happiness. My most heartfelt wish is that not one of my relations and connections may be missing at the final joyful reunion. (*Spiritual testament and final dispositions, Venice, June 29, 1954*)   —*JS*, 343

Go on loving one another, all you Roncallis, with the new families growing up among you, and try to understand that I cannot write to all separately. Our Giuseppino was right when he said to his brother the pope: "Here you are a prisoner *de luxe:* you cannot do all you would like to do."

I am well aware that you have to bear certain mortifications from people who like to talk nonsense. To have a pope in the family, a pope regarded with respect by the whole world, who yet permits his relations to go on living so modestly, in the same social condition as before! But many know that the pope, the son of humble but respected parents, never forgets anyone; he has, and shows, a great affection for his nearest kin; moreover, his own condition is the same as that of most of his recent predecessors; and a pope does not honor himself by enriching his relations but only by affectionately coming to their aid, according to their needs and the conditions of each one.

This is and will be one of the finest and most admired merits of Pope John and his Roncallis.

At my death I shall not lack the praise which did so much honor to the saintly Pius X: "He was born poor and died poor." (*Spiritual testament "to the Roncalli family," Vatican, December 3, 1961*)   —*JS*, 336

SAINTS CAN HAVE A SENSE OF HUMOR (STORIES ABOUT POPE JOHN)

Apprentice

Pope John found it very difficult to get used to some things required by Vatican protocol. For a long time he said "I" instead of "We" in his official talks. Popes are expected to use the royal "We," at least on official occasions. The hard task of being forced to use this form of address had come to him suddenly, and it frightened him a little. One day he looked through his slightly open door and saw a large number of visitors gathered in the antechamber. He braced himself, opened the door, and called out to the astonished group that they should please wait patiently just a little longer: "*Dio Mio!* So many people! Give me some time to learn the business of being Pope: Let me practice a little first!" — *PL,* 49

Family Audience

A few days after his coronation John held a special audience for his family, a privilege granted to each new occupant of St. Peter's Chair. The Roncallis entered the apartments in the apostolic palace timidly. The splendor of the place troubled their simple souls. Finally, bashful and confused, they stood before the white-clad figure of the pope. In their confusion they dropped their little presents. Peasant bread, ham, and wine, packed in brightly colored handkerchiefs, all tumbled to the floor. John looked at their staring eyes and open mouths. Although the comedy of the situation did not escape him, he spoke reassuringly: "Don't be afraid. It's only me." — *PL,* 53

Zeal

Ancient, weather-beating oaks flank the path in the higher part of
the Vatican gardens, where Pope Pius XII liked to stroll. Nearby
stands a fine marble bench surrounded by dense foliage and
shaded by a protecting crown of trees. John XXIII liked to go
to this refreshing spot, designed in the Italian style of the six-
teenth century. Not far away is a miniature grotto of Lourdes
sent by French Catholics to Leo XIII for the Vatican gardens.
One day John XXIII was accompanied to this inviting bench by
an eminent Canadian visitor. To break an uncomfortably long
silence, the visitor suddenly asked: "Holy Father, how many men
actually work at the Vatican?"

Not inclined to pursue a conversation at the time, Papa
Roncalli merely replied, "Half of them."   — *PL, 76*

Respect

One day Nuncio Roncalli met the chief rabbi of Paris and used the
occasion to show him his respect. It was at a diplomatic reception
which included the heads of all the different religious communities in Paris. In a long conversation which followed between
the two, they discovered that they had many things in common,
especially in terms of their human sympathies. When they were
finally summoned to dinner they suddenly found themselves —
still talking to each other with great interest and animation —
standing side by side directly in front of the entrance to the din-
ing hall. Nuncio Roncalli did not permit the ridiculous game of
"After you; no, after you" to drag on. He gently steered the chief
rabbi before him, saying: "The Old Testament before the New!"
— *PL, 95*

The Hat

At a fatiguing reception in Venice, Patriarch Roncalli held his hat in his hand. He saw no one among the many guests sipping cocktails with whom he was anxious to talk. He waited patiently for fifteen minutes, which he felt was required by politeness, before he could take his leave of the host. Suddenly one of the men who had arranged the party tried to take his hat. He wanted to hang it up in the closet. "No, no, leave it alone," resisted the patriarch, "you never know how useful it is on many occasions to have your hat in your hand." —*PL*, 109

Absent-Minded

During the nights following his election, Pope John XXIII was often unable to sleep. The immensity of the authority he had been given as visible head of five hundred million Catholics around the world brought him deep-rooted cares. He spoke of this later before a circle of visitors.

Many times he would scarcely fall asleep when some worry would seize him and wake him up again. One night when he was abruptly disturbed in slumber in this way, he mumbled: "I must talk this matter over with the pope." After a short pause of realization he rubbed his eyes and spoke to himself again in a louder voice. "The pope? *I'm* the pope. Well, then, I'll have to talk it over with the good Lord." —*PL*, 38

Lonely

A few weeks after his coronation, Pope John confided to his secretary, Capovilla, that he was unable to sleep through the night any more. He felt lonely, and this kept him awake. He needed more conversation and more social stimulation to help him lose the feeling of being deserted. The secretary was silent.

"Don't you think, Capovilla, that we might send for our good nuns from Bergamo?"

The little sisters were summoned. They not only took care of the pope's household; they cooked for the entire papal court. They knew what the pope liked to eat: simple, spicy foods. And their broad Bergamese dialect filled the apostolic palace with the conversation which the pope had missed.

But he still found it difficult to spend certain hours alone. He simply could not accustom himself to the habit of eating all by himself, a practice which Pius XII had always maintained. In a very short time Capovilla was invited to join him at the table. The pope's appetite improved immediately. Shortly afterward he invited the cardinals of the curia to be his table companions, one after the other. Little by little, bishops from all over the world, when they made their *ad limina* visits to Rome, were invited to join him for lunch or dinner.

Once a distinguished luncheon companion ventured to remind John of the solitary eating habits of Pius XII. "Well and good," John replied. "I value tradition and I grant that my predecessors did, too. I must confess, however, that I have never found any place in the Bible which suggests that the pope should eat alone."

—*PL, 29*

Humility

John XXIII paid considerable thought to all the problems which faced him. He gave his closest attention to every task or request, no matter how small. More than ever before in his life, John felt the responsibility that had been placed upon him in his position as pope. He did not feel it as a burden, as he often assured those around him, but more as a God-given mission, which he therefore carried out joyfully. For this reason John could surmount almost all difficulties with ease. His goodness used to turn opponents into repentant followers. He could never understand how men who held high office in the Church could complain about the burden of their pastoral and official tasks. Once a man is called by the Holy Spirit to be a priest, he used to say, he must assume the responsibility to preach and to practice the love of one's neighbor.

In the first private audience he had been granted, a newly appointed bishop complained to John XXIII that the added burden of his new office prevented him from sleeping. "Oh," said John compassionately, "the very same thing happened to me in the first few weeks of my pontificate, but then one day my guardian angel appeared to me in a daydream and whispered, 'Giovanni, don't take yourself so seriously.' And ever since then I've been able to sleep."   —*PL*, 85

The Vicar and the Mother Superior

One day John XXIII visited the Hospital of the Holy Spirit in Rome, which is administered by a religious sisterhood. The mother superior, deeply stirred by the papal visitation, went up to him in order to introduce herself:

"Most Holy Father, I am the Superior of the Holy Spirit!" she said.

"Well, I must say you're lucky," replied the pope. "I'm only the vicar of Jesus Christ!"   — *WW*, 72

Pope or Policeman

In the first days of his pontificate John XXIII received a letter from a twelve-year-old boy named Bruno. It read:

"My dear Pope: I am undecided. I want to be a policeman or a pope. What do you think?"

The pope replied:

"My little Bruno. If you want my opinion, learn how to be a policeman, because that cannot be improvised. As regards being pope, you will see later. Anybody can be pope; the proof of this is that I have become one. If you ever should be in Rome, come to see me. I would be glad to talk all this over with you."

— *WW*, 140

Shake Off the Imperial Dust

What did John XXIII expect from the Council? He explained himself profusely on this complex subject. But one day he made a gesture and uttered words that were eloquent in their Franciscan simplicity.

"The Council?" he said as he moved toward the window and made a gesture as if to open it. "I expect a little fresh air from it."

"We must shake off the imperial dust that has accumulated on the throne of St. Peter since Constantine." *(To an ambassador)*

— WW, 156–57

2

Transforming Leadership

Spiritual and political leaders, who have "principles" that keep changing according to changing circumstances and voters' moods, are not true leaders. Neither are true leaders those who talk the talk but do not walk the walk. Pope John XXIII was a master in true leadership. He listened to the Holy Spirit. He did not compromise with the truth. He underscored the responsibility of everyone — especially the media — in presenting the truth. He was clear about the hierarchy of values. He gave priority to love, peace, justice, and the common good. He showed us by his living example how to be the "good shepherd" and how the Church's authority is not a desire for power but for service. He lived what he preached, and he preached what he lived. On June 3, 1963, the day of Pope John's death, the archbishop of Milan, who would become Pope Paul VI, said, "Blessed be this pope who has enabled us to enjoy an hour of fatherly love and spiritual intimacy, and has taught us and the whole world that mankind needs nothing else so much as love" (JTP, 29). Pope John was certainly a good example to follow in his uncompromising love for God, the Church, and others. Also, he was a good example for those in positions of authority, who should be concerned first and foremost with doing God's will, discerning the signs of the times, and always opting to be on the side of true values and the common good by living them and implanting them.

WITNESSING TO THE TRUTH

I feel quite detached from everything, from all thought of advancement or anything else. I know I deserve nothing and I do not feel any impatience. It is true, however, that the difference between my way of seeing situations on the spot and certain ways of judging the same things in Rome hurts me considerably: it is my only real cross. I want to bear it humbly, with great willingness to please my principal Superiors, because this and nothing else is what I desire. I shall always speak the truth, but with mildness, keeping silence about what might seem a wrong or injury done to myself, ready to sacrifice myself or be sacrificed. The Lord sees everything and will deal justly with me. Above all, I wish to continue always to render good for evil, and in all things to endeavor to prefer the Gospel truth to the wiles of human politics. (*Retreat of October 13–16, 1936*)   —*JS*, 228

Ignorance of the Truth

All the evils which poison men and nations and trouble so many hearts have a single cause and a single source: ignorance of the truth — and at times even more than ignorance, a contempt for truth and a reckless rejection of it. Thus arise all manner of errors, which enter the recesses of men's hearts and the bloodstream of human society as would a plague. These errors turn everything upside down: they menace individuals and society itself.   —*APC*, 6

And yet, God gave each of us an intellect capable of attaining natural truth. If we adhere to this truth, we adhere to God himself, the author of truth, the lawgiver and ruler of our lives. But if we reject this truth, whether out of foolishness, neglect, or malice, we turn our backs on the highest good itself and on the very norm for right living.   —*APC*, 7

Revealed Truth

As We have said, it is possible for us to attain natural truth by virtue of our intellects. But all cannot do this easily; often their efforts will result in a mixture of truth and error. This is particularly the case in matters of religion and sound morals. Moreover, we cannot possibly attain those truths which exceed the capacity of nature and the grasp of reason, unless God enlightens and inspires us. This is why the word of God, "who dwells in light inaccessible" (1 Tim. 6:16), in his great love took pity on man's plight, "became flesh and dwelt among us" (John 1:14), that he might "enlighten every man who cometh into the world" (John 1:9) and lead him not only to full and perfect truth, but to virtue and eternal happiness. All men, therefore, are bound to accept the teaching of the Gospel. For if this is rejected, the very foundations of truth, goodness, and civilization are endangered. *— APC, 8*

Truth and Error

It is clear that We are discussing a serious matter, with which our eternal salvation is very intimately connected. Some men, as the Apostle of the Gentiles warns us, are "ever learning yet never attaining knowledge of the truth" (2 Tim. 3:7). They contend that the human mind can discover no truth that is certain or sure; they reject the truths revealed by God and necessary for our eternal salvation.

Such men have strayed pathetically far from the teaching of Christ and the views expressed by the Apostle when he said, "Let us all attain to the unity of the faith and of the deep knowledge of the Son of God . . . that we may no longer be children, tossed to and fro and carried about by every wind of doctrine devised in the wickedness of men, in craftiness, according to the wiles of error. Rather are we to practice the truth in love, and grow up in all things in him who is the head, Christ. For from him the whole body (being closely joined and knit together through every joint of the system according to the functioning in due measure of each single part) derives its increase to the building up of itself in love" (Eph. 4:13–16).

Anyone who consciously and wantonly attacks known truth, who arms himself with falsehood in his speech, his writings, or his conduct in order to attract and win over less learned men and to shape the inexperienced and impressionable minds of the young to his own way of thinking, takes advantage of the inexperience and innocence of others and engages in an altogether despicable business....

So much toil and effort is expended today in mastering and advancing human knowledge that our age glories — and rightly — in the amazing progress it has made in the field of scientific research. But why do we not devote as much energy, ingenuity, and enthusiasm to the sure and safe attainment of that learning which concerns not this earthly, mortal life but the life which lies ahead of us in heaven? Our spirit will rest in peace and joy only when we have reached that truth which is taught in the Gospels and which should be reduced to action in our lives. This is a joy which surpasses by far any pleasure which can come from the study of things human or from those marvelous inventions which we use today and are constantly praising to the skies.

Once we have attained the truth in its fullness, integrity, and purity, unity should pervade our minds, hearts, and actions. For there is only one cause of discord, disagreement, and dissension: ignorance of the truth, or what is worse, rejection of the truth once it has been sought and found. It may be that the truth is rejected because of the practical advantages which are expected to result from false views; it may be that it is rejected as a result of that perverted blindness which seeks easy and indulgent excuses for vice and immoral behavior.   — *APC*, 9–11, 19–20

Truth, Peace, Prosperity

All men, therefore, private citizens as well as government officials, must love the truth sincerely if they are to attain that peace and harmony on which depends all real prosperity, public and private. —*APC*, 21

A Self-Evident Truth

There is one truth especially which We think is self-evident: when the sacred rights of God and religion are ignored or infringed upon, the foundations of human society will sooner or later crumble and give way. Our predecessor of immortal memory, Leo XIII, expressed this truth well: "It follows...that law becomes ineffective and all authority is weakened once the sovereign and eternal rule of God, who commands and forbids, is rejected." Cicero expressed the same idea when he wrote, "You, the priests, are protecting Rome with religion more effectively than she is protected with walls."

As We reflect on these truths, We embrace with deep sorrow each and every one of the faithful who is impeded and restricted in the practice of his religion. They indeed often "suffer persecution for justice' sake" (Matt. 5:10), and for the sake of the kingdom of God. We share their sorrows, their hardships, their anxieties. We pray and beseech heaven to grant at length the dawn of a happier day. We earnestly desire all Our brethren in Christ and Our children throughout the world to join Us in this prayer. For thus a chorus of holy entreaties will rise from every nation to our merciful God and win a richer shower of graces for these unfortunate members of the mystical Body of Christ. —*APC*, 140–41

Witnesses to the Truth

Anyone who deems himself a Christian must know that he is bound by his conscience to the basic, imperative duty of bearing

witness to the truth in which he believes and to the grace which
has transformed his soul. A great Father of the Church has said:
"He [Christ] left us on earth in order that we should become
like beacons of light and teachers unto others; that we might
act like leaven, move among men like angels, be like men unto
children, and like spiritual men unto animal men, in order to
win them over, and that we may be like seed, and bear abundant
fruits. There would be no need for sermons, if our lives were
shining; there would be no need for words, if we bore witness
with our deeds. There would be no more pagans, if we were true
Christians" (St. John Chrysostom).   — *PP, 34*

False Philosophies

It must also be remarked that there are current today certain
schools of thought and philosophy and certain attitudes toward
the practical conduct of life which cannot possibly be reconciled
with the teachings of Christianity. This impossibility We shall
never cease from asserting in firm and unambiguous, though also
calm terms. But God wishes the welfare of men and of nations!

And so We hope that men will set aside those sterile postulates
and assumptions, hard as rock and just as inflexible, which rise
from a way of thinking and acting that is infected with laicism
and materialism, and that they will find a complete cure in that
sound doctrine which experience makes more certain with every
day that passes. We mean that doctrine which attests that God is
the author of life and its laws, that he is guarantor of the rights
and dignity of the human person. God then is "our refuge and
our Redemption" (Sacred Liturgy).   — *GR, 17–18*

The Coming of God's Kingdom

Our thoughts turn to all the lands of this earth. We see all mankind
striving for a better future; We see the awakening of a mysterious
force, and this permits Us to hope that men will be drawn by a

right conscience and a sense of duty to advance the real interests of human society. That this goal may be realized in the fullest sense — that is, with the triumph of the kingdom of truth, justice, peace, and charity — We exhort all Our children in Christ to be "of one heart and one soul" (Acts 4:32) and to pour out ardent prayers in October to our Queen in heaven and our loving Mother, reflecting upon the words of the Apostle: "In all things we suffer tribulation, but we are not distressed; we are sore pressed, but we are not destitute; we endure persecution, but we are not forsaken; we are cast down, but we do not perish; always bearing about in our body the dying of Jesus, so that the life also of Jesus may be made manifest in our bodily frame" (2 Cor 4:8–10).

— *GR*, 19

Mother and Teacher of all nations — such is the Catholic Church in the mind of her Founder, Jesus Christ; to hold the world in an embrace of love, that men, in every age, should find in her their own completeness in a higher order of living, and their ultimate salvation. She is "the pillar and ground of the truth" [see 1 Tim. 3:15]. To her was entrusted by her holy Founder the twofold task of giving life to her children and of teaching them and guiding them — both as individuals and as nations — with maternal care. Great is their dignity, a dignity which she has always guarded most zealously and held in the highest esteem.

Christianity is the meeting-point of earth and heaven. It lays claim to the whole man, body and soul, intellect and will, inducing him to raise his mind above the changing conditions of this earthly existence and reach upward for the eternal life of heaven, where one day he will find his unfailing happiness and peace.

— *MM*, 1–2

Temporal and Eternal

Hence, though the Church's first care must be for souls, how she can sanctify them and make them share in the gifts of heaven, she concerns herself too with the exigencies of man's daily life, with his livelihood and education, and his general, temporal welfare and prosperity.

In all this she is but giving effect to those principles which Christ himself established in the Church he founded. When he said "I am the way, and the truth, and the life" (John 14:6), "I am the light of the world" (John 8:12), it was doubtless man's eternal salvation that was uppermost in his mind, but he showed his concern for the material welfare of his people when, seeing the hungry crowd of his followers, he was moved to exclaim: "I have compassion on the multitude" (Mark 8:2). And these were no empty words of our divine Redeemer. Time and again he proved them by his actions, as when he miraculously multiplied bread to alleviate the hunger of the crowds.   — *MM*, 3–4

Mother and Teacher

For here Our concern is with the doctrine of the Catholic and Apostolic Church. She is the Mother and Teacher of all nations. Her light illumines, enkindles, and enflames. No age but hears her warning voice, vibrant with heavenly wisdom.

She is ever powerful to offer suitable, effective remedies for the increasing needs of men, and the sorrows and anxieties of this present life. Her words re-echo those of the Psalmist of old — words which never fail to raise our fainting spirits and give us courage: "I will hear what the Lord God will speak in me: for he will speak peace unto his people. And unto his saints: and unto them that are converted to the heart. Surely his salvation is near to them that fear him: that glory may dwell in our land. Mercy and truth have met each other: justice and peace have kissed. Truth is sprung out of the earth: and justice hath looked down from heaven. For the Lord will give goodness: and our earth shall yield her fruit. Justice shall walk before him: and shall set his steps in the way" (Ps. 84:9ff.)   — *MM*, 262

Social Life in Truth, Justice, Charity, and Freedom

Before a society can be considered well-ordered, creative, and consonant with human dignity, it must be based on truth. St. Paul expressed this as follows: "Putting away lying, speak ye the truth every man with his neighbor, for we are members one of another" [Eph. 4:25]. And so will it be, if each man acknowledges sincerely his own rights and his own duties toward others.

Human society, as We here picture it, demands that men be guided by justice, respect the rights of others, and do their duty. It demands, too, that they be animated by such love as will make them feel the needs of others as their own, and induce them to share their goods with others, and to strive in the world to make all men alike heirs to the noblest of intellectual and spiritual values. Nor is this enough; for human society thrives on freedom, namely, on the use of means which are consistent with the dignity of its individual members, who, being endowed with reason, assume responsibility for their own actions.

And so, dearest sons and brothers, we must think of human society as being primarily a spiritual reality. By its means enlightened men can share their knowledge of the truth, can claim their rights and fulfill their duties, receive encouragement in their aspirations for the goods of the spirit, share their enjoyment of all the wholesome pleasures of the world, and strive continually to pass on to others all that is best in themselves and to make their own the spiritual riches of others. It is these spiritual values which exert a guiding influence on culture, economics, social institutions, political movements and forms, laws, and all the other components which go to make up the external community of men and its continual development. — *PT,* 35–36

In Truth

The first point to be settled is that mutual ties between states must be governed by truth. Truth calls for the elimination of every trace of racial discrimination and the consequent recognition of the inviolable principle that all states are by nature equal in dignity.

Each of them accordingly has the right to exist, to develop, and to possess the necessary means and accept a primary responsibility for its own development. Each is also legitimately entitled to its good name and to the respect which is its due.

As we know from experience, men frequently differ widely in knowledge, virtue, intelligence, and wealth, but that is no valid argument in favor of a system whereby those who are in a position of superiority impose their will arbitrarily on others. On the contrary, such men have a greater share in the common responsibility to help others to reach perfection by their mutual efforts.

So, too, on the international level: some nations may have attained to a superior degree of scientific, cultural and economic development. But that does not entitle them to exert unjust political domination over other nations. It means that they have to make a greater contribution to the common cause of social progress.

The fact is that no one can be by nature superior to his fellows, since all men are equally noble in natural dignity. And consequently there are no differences at all between political communities from the point of view of natural dignity. Each state is like a body, the members of which are human beings. And, as we know from experience, nations can be highly sensitive in matters in any way touching their dignity and honor; and with good reason.   — PT, 86–89

The Question of Propaganda

Truth further demands an attitude of unruffled impartiality in the use of the many aids to the promotion and spread of mutual understanding between nations which modern scientific progress has made available. This does not mean that people should be prevented from drawing particular attention to the virtues of their own way of life, but it does mean the utter rejection of ways of disseminating information which violate the principles of truth and justice, and injure the reputation of another nation. — *PT*, 90

Error and the Errant

It is always perfectly justifiable to distinguish between error as such and the person who falls into error — even in the case of men who err regarding the truth or are led astray as a result of their inadequate knowledge, in matters either of religion or of the highest ethical standards. A man who has fallen into error does not cease to be a man. He never forfeits his personal dignity; and that is something that must always be taken into account. Besides, there exists in man's very nature an undying capacity to break through the barriers of error and seek the road to truth. God, in his great providence, is ever present with his aid. Today, maybe, a man lacks faith and turns aside into error; tomorrow, perhaps, illumined by God's light, he may indeed embrace the truth.

Catholics who, in order to achieve some external good, collaborate with unbelievers or with those who through error lack the fullness of faith in Christ, may possibly provide the occasion or even the incentive for their conversion to the truth. — *PT*, 158

Philosophies and Historical Movements

Again it is perfectly legitimate to make a clear distinction between a false philosophy of the nature, origin and purpose of men and the world, and economic, social, cultural, and political undertakings, even when such undertakings draw their origin and inspiration from that philosophy. True, the philosophic formula does not change once it has been set down in precise terms, but the undertakings clearly cannot avoid being influenced to a certain extent by the changing conditions in which they have to operate. Besides, who can deny the possible existence of good and commendable elements in these undertakings, elements which do indeed conform to the dictates of right reason, and are an expression of man's lawful aspirations?

It may sometimes happen, therefore, that meetings arranged for some practical end — though hitherto they were thought to be altogether useless — may in fact be fruitful at the present time, or at least offer prospects of success. But whether or not the moment for such cooperation has arrived, and the manner and degree of such cooperation in the attainment of economic, social, cultural, and political advantages — these are matters for prudence to decide; prudence, the queen of all the virtues which rule the lives of men both as individuals and in society.

As far as Catholics are concerned, the decision rests primarily with those who take a leading part in the life of the community, and in these specific fields. They must, however, act in accordance with the principles of the natural law and observe the Church's social teaching and the directives of ecclesiastical authority. For it must not be forgotten that the Church has the right and duty not only to safeguard her teaching on faith and morals, but also to exercise her authority over her sons by intervening in their external affairs whenever a judgment has to be made concerning the practical application of this teaching.   — *PT,* 159–60

Mgr. Guerry, archbishop of Cambrai, tells us:

On May 3, last year, in private conversation, the pope confided to me his grief that so many men of good will in the world thought that the Church rejected and condemned them. Then, showing me the crucifix upon his table, he said with emotion: "But I must be like Christ. I open wide my arms to embrace them. I love them and I am their father. I am always ready to welcome them." Then, turning to me, he said: "Monsignore, all that the Gospel requires of us has not yet been understood."   — *JTP,* 31

TRUE LEADERS RESPECT
THE HIERARCHY OF VALUES

Equality of Men

Today ... the conviction is widespread that all men are equal in natural dignity; and so, on the doctrinal and theoretical level, at least, no form of approval is being given to racial discrimination. All this is of supreme significance for the formation of a human society animated by the principles We have mentioned above, for man's awareness of his rights must inevitably lead him to the recognition of his duties. The possession of rights involves the duty of implementing those rights, for they are the expression of a man's personal dignity. And the possession of rights also involves their recognition and respect by other people.

When society is formed on a basis of rights and duties, men have an immediate grasp of spiritual and intellectual values, and have no difficulty in understanding what is meant by truth, justice, charity, and freedom. They become, moreover, conscious of being members of such a society. And that is not all. Inspired by such principles, they attain to a better knowledge of the true God — a personal God transcending human nature. They recognize that their relationship with God forms the very foundation of their life — the interior life of the spirit, and the life which they live in the society of their fellows. — *PT,* 44–45

Respecting a Nation's Individuality

The developing nations, obviously, have certain unmistakable characteristics of their own, resulting from the nature of the particular region and the natural dispositions of their citizens, with their time-honored traditions and customs.

In helping these nations, therefore, the more advanced communities must recognize and respect this individuality. They must beware of making the assistance they give an excuse for forcing these people into their own national mold.   — MM, 169–70

Respecting the True Hierarchy of Values

Scientific and technical progress, economic development and the betterment of living conditions, are certainly valuable elements in a civilization. But we must realize that they are essentially instrumental in character. They are not supreme values in themselves.

It pains Us, therefore, to observe the complete indifference to the true hierarchy of values shown by so many people in the economically developed countries. Spiritual values are ignored, forgotten, or denied, while the progress of science, technology, and economics is pursued for its own sake, as though material well-being were the be-all and end-all of life. This attitude is contagious, especially when it infects the work that is being done for the less developed countries, which have often preserved in their ancient traditions an acute and vital awareness of the more important human values, on which the moral order rests.

To attempt to undermine this national integrity is clearly immoral. It must be respected and as far as possible clarified and developed, so that it may remain what it is: a foundation of true civilization.   — MM, 175–77

Spiritual and Moral Values

The almost limitless horizons opened up by scientific research only go to confirm this truth. More and more men are beginning to realize that science has so far done little more than scratch the surface of nature and reality. There are vast hidden depths still to be explored and adequately explained. Such men are appalled when they consider how these gigantic forces for good can be turned by science into engines of destruction. They realize then the supreme importance of spiritual and moral values, if scientific and technical progress is to be used in the service of civilization, and not involve the whole human race in irremediable disaster.

Furthermore, the increasing sense of dissatisfaction with worldly goods which is making itself felt among citizens of the wealthier nations, is rapidly destroying the treasured illusion of an earthly paradise. Men, too, are becoming more and more conscious of their rights as human beings, rights which are universal and inviolable; and they are aspiring to more just and more human relations with their fellows. The effect of all this is to make the modern man more deeply aware of his own limitations, and to create in him a striving for spiritual values. All of which encourages Us in the hope that individuals and nations will one day learn to unite in a spirit of sincere understanding and profitable cooperation.   — *MM*, 210–11

True Hierarchy of Values

In Our paternal care as universal Pastor of souls, We earnestly beg Our sons, immersed though they be in the business of this world, not to allow their consciences to sleep; not to lose sight of the true hierarchy of values.

Certainly, the Church teaches — and has always taught — that scientific and technical progress and the resultant material well-being are good things and mark an important phase in human civilization. But the Church teaches, too, that goods of this kind must be valued according to their true nature: as instruments used by man for the better attainment of his end. They help to make him a better man, both in the natural and the supernatural order.

May these warning words of the divine Master ever sound in men's ears: "For what doth it profit a man, if he gain the whole world and suffer the loss of his own soul? Or what exchange shall a man give for his soul?" (Matt. 16:26). — *MM*, 245–47

It is only when the dignity of the person comes to be taken as the standard of value for man and his activities that the means will exist to settle civil discord and the often profound divisions between, for example, employers and the employed. Above all, it is only then that the means will exist to secure for the institution of the family those conditions of life, work, and assistance which are capable of making it better directed to its function as a cell of society and the first community instituted by God himself for the development of the human person.   — CM

TRUE LEADERS TALK THE TALK
AND WALK THE WALK

Stories of Pope John

The most recent predecessors of Pope John XXIII preferred to take their strolls in the Vatican gardens undisturbed. At most, they allowed one of their secretaries to accompany them. Just before the pope appeared, always at a definite time, the gardeners and other workers on the grounds would withdraw.

But Pope John liked to take unannounced walks. The first time, all the workers were startled when they suddenly saw the pope approach. Later, a fundamental change was adopted in this regard, as it was in many other practices. But this first encounter was a subject of amusement to the pope. A group of street cleaners took to flight as if they were retreating from a leper. Each man tried to hide, some behind bushes, others behind a projecting wall.

The pope did not enjoy this game of hide-and-seek. "Come out again, all of you," he called out. "I won't do anything to you. I want to talk to you. Come. Hurry up, *avante, venite!*" Timidly, and very slowly, one after another, they came up to the pope. He did not let them stay on their knees very long, but instead asked them about their families. After they had all had the chance to boast that they were the fathers of a fairly large number of children, John said, "There were twelve children in our home, too. They are all farmers except myself. Five of them are still living." Then the pope wanted to know what they received as wages for their work. "What?" he replied, frowning, when they told him that they made only 1,000 lire a day ($1.60). "That's only 24,000 lire a month ($38.40). No family with lots of children can live on that. What has become of justice? Just wait, we'll change that."

The pope turned around and went immediately to his study to investigate. First he canceled the contract with the Roman firm which, in a written agreement for the cleaning and maintenance of Vatican streets also stipulated the small salaries given the workers. Considering the fees mentioned in the contract, the company certainly should have been able to pay higher wages.

This marked the beginning of a general review of all wage and salary scales in the Vatican. The lowest wages were doubled, while the higher ones were increased in a gradually decreasing scale, so that today the wages and salaries in the Vatican are significantly higher than those in the rest of Italy. At the same time, the pope ordered that for each child a man had, he should receive an extra monthly allowance of 10,000 lira. It is not surprising that Roman workers now compete for jobs in the Vatican, which only recently they scorned.

When the pope announced these decrees, affecting almost three thousand salaried workers in the Vatican, he counseled their administrators in these words: "We cannot always require others to observe the Church's teaching on social justice if we do not apply it in our own domain. The Church must take the lead in social justice by its own good example."   —*PL,* 47–48

"I Shall Not Ask You Whether You Are a Catholic"

A legend narrates that Constantine the Great, when leaving Rome for the East, said: "My Rome is Sardica," for he intended to found in what is today the capital of Bulgaria the majestic capital of his Empire of the East. Later on, however, after arriving here, he changed his plan and went on to the shores of the Bosphorus, where he built the great city which has borne his name through the centuries. It has fallen to me to follow the path of Constantine, although in a much more modest way; the way, I mean, from Sardica to Constantinople, from Sofia to Istanbul. However, as I leave for my new destination I carry with me a precious memory of Bulgaria. I have begged the Holy Father to be good enough to change my archbishop's title to that of a wonderful place, a delightful place in Bulgaria. From now onward I shall no longer bear the name of archbishop of Aeropolis, but that of archbishop of Mesembria. In this way I shall have something to remind me every day of Bulgaria, a memory which will stir my heart every time I raise my hand to bless the people in solemn moments, and every time I set my signature to a document.

But you also, brothers, on whom my blessing rests, do not forget me; I wish to remain your friend forever, the firm and loving friend of Bulgaria.

According to a tradition still preserved in Catholic Ireland, on Christmas Eve every house sets a light in the window, in order to let Joseph and Mary know, in case they are passing by that night looking for shelter, that inside there is a family, awaiting them around the fire and around the table laden with the gifts of God. Dear brothers, no one knows the ways of the future! Wherever I might go in the world, if someone from Bulgaria should pass by my house, at night, in distress, he will find a lamp lit in my window. Knock! Knock! I will not ask you if you are a Catholic or not; it is enough that you are my brother from Bulgaria: enter! Two brotherly arms will embrace you, the warm heart of a friend will welcome you. For such is the Christian charity of the Lord, expressions of which have sweetened my life during my ten years sojourn in Bulgaria. (*Farewell speech to the Bulgarian people,* 1934)
                                                         —*JTP,* 168–69

"We Did Not Discuss, but We Became Fond of Each Other"

Dear Gentlemen, our meeting today, so welcome to all, has a family air, a note of confidence: it is to be marked by respect and simplicity.

The first thought that rises from my heart is a prayer; it is a useful lesson to all, taken from Psalm 67: "Blessed is the Lord who daily bears us up; God is our salvation" (Ps. 67 [68]:19).

In 1952 Pope Pius XII, with an unforeseen and surprising gesture, asked me to become patriarch of Venice. I told him that I did not need much time for reflection before accepting. In fact my own will did not enter into this proposal at all; there was in my mind no desire to be directed to this rather than to any other ministry or office.

My episcopal motto was a sufficient answer: Obedience and Peace!

When then, after thirty years of service under the direct orders of the Holy See, I prepared to start an almost new kind of life and meet the people of Venice, whom I was to lead for six years as their pastor, I thought over and meditated these words of the Psalm: "God bears us up." He bears us up as we are, and with what we have: with the wealth he gives us and the poverty we create for ourselves.

This same thought was with me when four years ago I accepted the succession to St. Peter, and has been with me in all that has been done since then, day by day, until the announcement and the beginning of the Council.

As far as my humble person is concerned I do not like to speak of special inspirations. I hold to sound doctrine: it teaches me that everything comes from God. In this perspective I have been able to consider as heavenly inspiration also the idea of the Council, which was opened on the October 11.

I can assure you that I was full of emotion on that day. In that God-given and historic hour I was above all careful to do my immediate duty, which was to remain collected, to pray, and to thank the Lord. But every now and then my eyes turned to all my sons and brothers. And when my glance fell on your group, on each one of you, I found that your presence gave me joy.

Without wishing to anticipate the results, let us be content today to state the facts. Blessed be God for each day as it comes.

As far as you yourselves are concerned, look into my heart: you will perhaps find there much more than my words can tell you.

How can I forget the ten years I passed at Sofia? And the ten more years passed at Istanbul and Athens? They were twenty happy and well spent years, during which I made the acquaintance of venerable personalities as well as of many generous young people. I observed them with affectionate respect, even if my mission as representative of the Holy See in the Near East did not directly concern them.

Then in Paris, which is one of the most typically cosmopolitan centers, and this was particularly true immediately after the last war, I was able to meet innumerable Christians belonging to various denominations.

We did not debate, we talked; we did not discuss, but we became fond of each other!

One day long ago I handed to a venerable old man, the prelate of an Eastern Church not in communion with Rome, a medal of the pontificate of Pius XI. The gesture was intended as, and was indeed, a simple act of affectionate courtesy. Sometime afterward the old man, about to close his eyes to the light of this world, desired that when he died this medal should be placed on his heart. I saw this with my own eyes, and the memory still moves me.

I have alluded to this episode on purpose. In its touching simplicity it is like a wild flower: as the new season returns, it can once more be plucked, and offered. (*Speech to the Observers, October 13, 1962*)   —*JTP*, 269–71

TRUE LEADERS STAND
FOR THE COMMON GOOD

Attainment of the Common Good Is the Purpose of the Public Authority

Men, both as individuals and as intermediate groups, are required to make their own specific contributions to the general welfare. The main consequence of this is that they must harmonize their own interests with the needs of others, and offer their goods and services as their rulers shall direct — assuming, of course, that justice is maintained and the authorities are acting within the limits of their competence. Those who have authority in the state must exercise that authority in a way which is not only morally irreproachable, but also best calculated to ensure or promote the state's welfare.

The attainment of the common good is the sole reason for the existence of civil authorities. In working for the common good, therefore, the authorities must obviously respect its nature, and at the same time adjust their legislation to meet the requirements of the given situation. — *PT, 53–54*

Essentials of the Common Good

Among the essential elements of the common good one must certainly include the various characteristics distinctive of each individual people. But these by no means constitute the whole of it. For the common good, since it is intimately bound up with human nature, can never exist fully and completely unless the human person is taken into account at all times. Thus, attention must be paid to the basic nature of the common good and what it is that brings it about.

We must add, therefore, that it is in the nature of the common good that every single citizen has the right to share in it — although in different ways, depending on his tasks, merits, and circumstances. Hence every civil authority must strive to promote the common good in the interest of all, without favoring any individual citizen or category of citizen. As Pope Leo XIII insisted: "The civil power must not be subservient to the advantage of any one individual, or of some few persons; inasmuch as it was established for the common good of all."

Nevertheless, considerations of justice and equity can at times demand that those in power pay more attention to the weaker members of society, since these are at a disadvantage when it comes to defending their own rights and asserting their legitimate interests.   — *PT,* 55–56

The Spiritual, Too

In this connection, We would draw the attention of Our own sons to the fact that the common good is something which affects the needs of the whole man, body and soul. That, then, is the sort of good which rulers of states must take suitable measure to ensure. They must respect the hierarchy of values and aim at achieving the spiritual as well as the material prosperity of their subjects.

These principles are clearly contained in that passage in Our encyclical *Mater et Magistra* where We emphasized that the common good "must take account of all those social conditions which favor the full development of human personality."

Consisting, as he does, of body and immortal soul, man cannot in this mortal life satisfy his needs or attain perfect happiness. Thus, the measures that are taken to implement the common good must not jeopardize his eternal salvation; indeed, they must even help him to obtain it.   — *PT,* 57–59

Responsibilities of the Public Authority, and Rights and Duties of Individuals

It is generally accepted today that the common good is best safeguarded when personal rights and duties are guaranteed. The chief concern of civil authorities must therefore be to ensure that these rights are recognized, respected, coordinated, defended, and promoted, and that each individual is enabled to perform his duties more easily. For "to safeguard the inviolable rights of the human person, and to facilitate the performance of his duties, is the principal duty of every public authority."

Thus any government which refused to recognize human rights or acted in violation of them, would not only fail in its duty; its decrees would be wholly lacking in binding force. — *PT,* 60–61

Contacts between Races

Furthermore, the universal common good requires the encouragement in all nations of every kind of reciprocation between citizens and their intermediate societies. There are many parts of the world where we find groupings of people of more or less different ethnic origin. Nothing must be allowed to prevent reciprocal relations between them. Indeed such a prohibition would flout the very spirit of an age which has done so much to nullify the distances separating peoples.

Nor must one overlook the fact that whatever their ethnic background, men possess, besides the special characteristics which distinguish them from other men, other very important elements in common with the rest of mankind. And these can form the basis of their progressive development and self-realization especially in regard to spiritual values. They have, therefore, the right and duty to carry on their lives with others in society. — *PT,* 100

Connection between the Common Good and Political Authority

Now, if one considers carefully the inner significance of the common good on the one hand, and the nature and function of public authority on the other, one cannot fail to see that there is an intrinsic connection between them. Public authority, as the means

of promoting the common good in civil society, is a postulate of
the moral order. But the moral order likewise requires that this
authority be effective in attaining its end. Hence the civil institutions in which such authority resides, becomes operative, and
promotes its ends are endowed with a certain kind of structure
and efficacy: a structure and efficacy which make such institutions capable of realizing the common good by ways and means
adequate to the changing historical conditions.

Today the universal common good presents us with problems
which are worldwide in their dimensions; problems, therefore,
which cannot be solved except by a public authority with power,
organization, and means co-extensive with these problems, and
with a worldwide sphere of activity. Consequently the moral
order itself demands the establishment of some such general form
of public authority.   —*PT*, 136–37

Public Authority Instituted by Common Consent and Not Imposed by Force

But this general authority equipped with worldwide power and
adequate means for achieving the universal common good cannot
be imposed by force. It must be set up with the consent of all
nations. If its work is to be effective, it must operate with fairness,
absolute impartiality, and dedication to the common good of all
peoples. The forcible imposition by the more powerful nations
of a universal authority of this kind would inevitably arouse
fears of its being used as an instrument to serve the interests
of the few or to take the side of a single nation, and thus the
influence and effectiveness of its activity would be undermined.
For even though nations may differ widely in material progress
and military strength, they are very sensitive as regards their
juridical equality and the excellence of their own way of life. They
are right, therefore, in their reluctance to submit to an authority
imposed by force, established without their cooperation, or not
accepted of their own accord.   —*PT*, 138

The Universal Common Good and Personal Rights

The common good of individual states is something that cannot be determined without reference to the human person, and the same is true of the common good of all states taken together. Hence the public authority of the world community must likewise have as its special aim the recognition, respect, safeguarding, and promotion of the rights of the human person. This can be done by direct action, if need be, or by the creation throughout the world of the sort of conditions in which rulers of individual states can more easily carry out their specific functions.   —*PT,* 139

The State's Role

As for the state, its whole raison d'être is the realization of the common good in the temporal order. It cannot, therefore, hold aloof from economic matters. On the contrary, it must do all in its power to promote the production of a sufficient supply of material goods, "the use of which is necessary for the practice of virtue" (St. Thomas, *De regimine principum,* I, 15). It has also the duty to protect the rights of all its people, and particularly of its weaker members, the workers, women, and children. It can never be right for the state to shirk its obligation of working actively for the betterment of the condition of the workingman.

It is furthermore the duty of the state to ensure that terms of employment are regulated in accordance with justice and equity, and to safeguard the human dignity of workers by making sure that they are not required to work in an environment which may prove harmful to their material and spiritual interests. It was for this reason that the Leonine encyclical enunciated those general principles of rightness and equity which have been assimilated into the social legislation of many a modern state, and which, as Pope Pius XI declared in the encyclical *Quadragesimo Anno,* have made no small contribution to the rise and development of that new branch of jurisprudence called labor law.   —*MM,* 20–21

The Demands of the Common Good

But a further point needs emphasizing: Any adjustment between
wages and profits must take into account the demands of the
common good of the particular country and of the whole human
family.

What are these demands? On the national level they include:
employment of the greatest possible number of workers; care lest
privileged classes arise, even among the workers; maintenance of
equilibrium between wages and prices; the need to make goods
and services accessible to the greatest number; elimination, or at
least the restriction, or inequalities in the various branches of the
economy — that is, between agriculture, industry and services;
creation of a proper balance between economic expansion and
the development of social services, especially through the activity
of public authorities; the best possible adjustment of the means
of production to the progress of science and technology; seeing
to it that the benefits which make possible a more human way
of life will be available not merely to the present generation but
to the coming generations as well.

The demands of the common good on the international level
include: the avoidance of all forms of unfair competition between
the economies of different countries; the fostering of mutual
collaboration and good will; and effective cooperation in the
development of economically less advanced communities.

These demands of the common good, both on a national and
a world level, must also be borne in mind when assessing the rate
of return due as compensation to the company's management,
and as interest or dividends to investors.   — MM, 78–81

The Common Good

The justification of all government action is the common good.
Public authority, therefore, must bear in mind the interests of
the state as a whole; which means that it must promote all three

areas of production — agriculture, industry, and services — simultaneously and evenly. Everything must be done to ensure that citizens of the less developed areas are treated as responsible human beings and are allowed to play the major role in achieving their own economic, social, and cultural advancement.

— MM, 151

The Concept of Authority

Whoever is invested with authority, understood in its true meaning of a mission and a service, must try to realize what God is asking of him, and to make God's will the mainspring of all his thoughts and actions.

This must be so: human life must be an expression of the will of God, shown in obedience to the commandments engraved on men's hearts and revealed in the two Testaments which Christ entrusted to his Church.

And Christian living is living according to the will of God, sublimely revealed in the teaching of the Gospel, that "good news" which reverses our merely earthly way of judging things and events. What words these are, my dear people! "Blessed are the poor, blessed are the meek, blessed are the merciful, the pure in heart, the peacemakers; blessed are those who mourn and those who hunger and thirst for righteousness" (see Matt. 5:3–10).

These are the principles which offer the motives and ideals for a Christian life here below.

Human society means generous service to our fellows, a service which draws its inspiration from the order of the created world and is unwearied because it feels an imperative need to spend itself in accordance with the Pauline expression: "The love of Christ controls us" (2 Cor. 5:14). In this way it cooperates in that wise, liberal, and willing evolution which is derived — allow me to say this — clearly and authoritatively from the social teaching of the Christian Church. *— PD, 178–79*

The Right Use of Authority

Authority is not an uncontrolled force: it is the right to rule according to reason. Therefore it derives its power to command from the moral order which is founded on God, its first principle and its last end.

Authority which is based mainly or only on the threats and fear of punishment, or on the promise and expectation of reward, is not an effective means of making human beings work for the common good. Even if it were to succeed the result would not be consonant with the personal dignity of the subject, that of a free and reasonable being. Authority is essentially a moral force; therefore it must make its appeal primarily to the conscience, the sense of duty which everyone must willingly obey as his contribution to the good of all. Human beings are all equal in their natural dignity: none may penetrate to the interior life of another. This only God can do, because he alone sees and judges the intentions of our innermost soul.

Human authority can therefore be a moral obligation only if it is intrinsically in harmony with the authority of God and has a share in this. In this way the personal dignity of citizens is safeguarded, since their obedience to the public authorities is not the subjection of one man to another but, in its true significance, an act of homage to God, our provident Creator, who has decreed that the conditions of social life shall be regulated according to an order he himself has instituted. There is no humiliation in rendering homage to God; in fact this raises and ennobles us, for "to serve God is to reign."   —*PD*, 163–64

TRUE LEADERS DISCERN
THE SIGNS OF THE TIMES

Indeed, we make ours the recommendation of Jesus that one should know how to distinguish the "signs of the times" (Matt.

16:4), and we seem to see now, in the midst of so much darkness, a few indications which augur well for the fate of the Church and of humanity.

The bloody wars that have followed one on the other in our times, the spiritual ruins caused by many ideologies, and the fruits of so many bitter experiences have not been without useful teachings. Scientific progress itself, which gave man the possibility of creating catastrophic instruments for his destruction, has raised questions. It has obliged human beings to become thoughtful, more conscious of their own limitations, desirous of peace, and attentive to the importance of spiritual values. And it has accelerated that progress of closer collaboration and of mutual integration toward which, even though in the midst of a thousand uncertainties, the human family seems to be moving. And this facilitates, no doubt, the apostolate of the Church, since many people who did not realize the importance of its mission in the past are, taught by experience, today more disposed to welcome its warnings.

Then, if we turn our attention to the Church, we see that it has not remained a lifeless spectator in the face of these events, but has followed step by step the evolution of peoples, scientific progress, and social revolution. It has opposed decisively the materialistic ideologies which deny faith. Lastly, it has witnessed the rise and growth of the immense energies of the apostolate of prayer, of action in all fields. It has seen the emergence of a clergy constantly better equipped in learning and virtue for its mission, and of a laity which has become ever more conscious of its responsibilities within the bosom of the Church, and, in a special way, of its duty to collaborate with the Church hierarchy.

To this should be added the immense suffering of entire Christian communities, through which a multitude of admirable bishops, priests, and laymen seal their adherence to the faith, bearing persecutions of all kinds and revealing forms of heroism which certainly equal those of the most glorious periods of the Church.

Thus, though the world may appear profoundly changed, the Christian community is also in great part transformed and renewed. It has therefore strengthened itself socially in unity; it has been reinvigorated intellectually; it has been interiorly purified and is thus ready for trial.   — *DV,* 704–5

Characteristics of the Present Day

There are three things which characterize our modern age.

In the first place we notice a progressive improvement in the economic and social condition of working men. They began by claiming their rights principally in the economic and social spheres, and then proceeded to lay claim to their political rights as well. Finally, they have turned their attention to acquiring the more cultural benefits of society.

Today, therefore, working men all over the world are loud in their demands that they shall in no circumstances be subjected to arbitrary treatment, as though devoid of intelligence and freedom. They insist on being treated as human beings, with a share in every sector of human society: in the socio-economic sphere, in government, and in the realm of learning and culture.

Secondly, the part that women are now playing in political life is everywhere evident. This is a development that is perhaps of swifter growth among Christian nations, but it is also happening extensively, if more slowly, among nations that are heirs to different traditions and imbued with a different culture. Women are gaining an increasing awareness of their natural dignity. Far from being content with a purely passive role or allowing themselves to be regarded as a kind of instrument, they are demanding both in domestic and in public life the rights and duties which belong to them as human persons.

Finally, we are confronted in this modern age with a form of society which is evolving on entirely new social and political lines. Since all peoples have either attained political independence or are on the way to attaining it, soon no nation will rule over another and none will be subject to an alien power.

Thus all over the world men are either the citizens of an independent state, or are shortly to become so; nor is any nation nowadays content to submit to foreign domination. The long-standing inferiority complex of certain classes because of their economic and social status, sex, or position in the state, and the corresponding superiority complex of other classes, is rapidly becoming a thing of the past. —*PT*, 39–43

3

The Church in the Modern World

The Second Vatican Council was one of the greatest events in the history of Christianity. It was great not because it made possible certain changes in the way we worship or perform religious duties. It was especially great because it allowed us to change the way we think and perceive things. Now, with the inspiration of the Holy Spirit, we may be able to read history with more humility so that we can work more seriously to achieve Christian unity. Now every one of us feels more obligated than ever before to participate more directly in the work of the kingdom of God. Now, as the "people of God," we have the duty to live and preach the Gospel in any place and under any circumstance of our lives. Now, we become more aware than ever before that holiness is not the monopoly of bishops, priests, monks, and nuns, but it is everyone's call. Pope John XXIII allowed this perception to form. He did not necessarily dictate all the changes that occurred. But he provided the climate and conditions that can generate them. He set the stage for them to take shape. If some may still mourn the loss of the old Catholic identity, putting the blame on the Second Vatican Council and the pope who convoked it, they do it because of a certain way of seeing things that is valid in essence but too limited in scope. A more genuine Catholic identity, as Pope John showed, springs from within the Gospel truth where all of us should find our true selves as the beloved children of God. Indeed, beneath

the surface there is that deeper Self — the Source and Truth of our being — that helps us to unceasingly re-prioritize all the levels of our lives in alignment with the Word of God that is continuously working in and through us.

THE SECOND VATICAN COUNCIL

Prayer and Penance for the Coming Council

We too, Venerable Brethren, on the example of Our predecessors, are most anxious that the whole Catholic world, both clerical and lay, shall prepare itself for this great event, the forthcoming Council, by ardent prayer, good works, and the practice of Christian penance.

Clearly the most efficacious kind of prayer for gaining the divine protection is prayer that is offered publicly by the whole community; for Our Redeemer said: "Where two or three are gathered together for my sake, there am I in the midst of them" (Matt. 18:20).

The situation, therefore, demands that Christians today, as in the days of the early Church, shall be of "one heart and one soul" (Acts 4:32), imploring God with prayer and penance to grant that this great assembly may measure up to all our expectations.

The salutary results we pray for are these: that the faith, the love, the moral lives of Catholics may be so reinvigorated, so intensified, that all who are at present separated from this Apostolic See may be impelled to strive actively and sincerely for union, and enter the one fold under the one Shepherd (see John 10:16). . . .

"Behold, now is the acceptable time; behold, now is the day of salvation" (2 Cor. 6:2). These are words which We consider most applicable to that period of time which will shortly be upon us when the Ecumenical Council is in session. But when God in his providence decrees to give his supernatural gifts to men, he does so in the measure of their own individual desires and dispositions. Hence Our long-continued insistence on the spiritual preparation of Christians for this great event. Hence, too, the supreme importance of giving heed to this final invitation of Ours addressed to those who are willing to be guided by Our demands.   — *PA*, 22–25, 39

The greatest concern of the Ecumenical Council is this: that the sacred deposit of Christian doctrine should be guarded and taught more efficaciously. That doctrine embraces the whole of man, composed as he is of body and soul. And, since he is a pilgrim on this earth, it commands him to tend always toward heaven.

This demonstrates how our mortal life is to be ordered in such a way as to fulfill our duties as citizens of earth and of heaven, and thus to attain the aim of life as established by God. That is, all men, whether taken singly or as united in society, today have the duty of tending ceaselessly during their lifetime toward the attainment of heavenly things and to use, for this purpose only, the earthly goods, the employment of which must not prejudice their eternal happiness.

The Lord has said: "Seek first the kingdom of God and his justice" (Matt. 6:33). The word "first" expresses the direction in which our thoughts and energies must move. We must not, however, neglect the other words of this exhortation of our Lord, namely: "And all these things shall be given you besides." In reality, there always have been in the Church, and there are still today, those who, while seeking the practice of evangelical perfection with all their might, do not fail to make themselves useful to society. Indeed, it is from their constant example of life and their charitable undertakings that all that is highest and noblest in human society takes its strength and growth.

In order, however, that this doctrine may influence the numerous fields of human activity, with reference to individuals, to families, and to social life, it is necessary first of all that the Church should never depart from the sacred patrimony of truth received from the Fathers. But at the same time she must ever look to the present, to the new conditions and new forms of life introduced into the modern world which have opened new avenues to the Catholic apostolate....

The substance of the ancient doctrine of the deposit of faith is one thing, and the way in which it is presented is another. And it is the latter that must be taken into great consideration with patience if necessary, everything being measured in the forms and proportions of a magisterium which is predominantly pastoral in character.

At the outset of the Second Vatican Council, it is evident, as always, that the truth of the Lord will remain forever. We see, in fact, as one age succeeds another, that the opinions of men follow one another and exclude each other. And often errors vanish as quickly as they arise, like fog before the sun.

The Church has always opposed these errors. Frequently she has condemned them with the greatest severity. Nowadays, however, the Spouse of Christ prefers to make use of the medicine of mercy rather than that of severity. She considers that she meets the needs of the present day by demonstrating the validity of her teaching rather than by condemnations. Not, certainly, that there is a lack of fallacious teaching, opinions, and dangerous concepts to be guarded against and dissipated. But these are so obviously in contrast with the right norm of honesty, and have produced such lethal fruits, that by now it would seem that men of themselves are inclined to condemn them, particularly those ways of life which despise God and his law or place excessive confidence in technical progress and a well-being based exclusively on the comforts of life. They are ever more deeply convinced of the paramount dignity of the human person and of his perfections, as well as of the duties which that implies. Even more important, experience has taught men that violence inflicted on others, the might of arms, and political domination are of no help at all in finding a happy solution to the grave problems which afflict them.

That being so, the Catholic Church, raising the torch of religious truth by means of this Ecumenical Council, desires to show

herself to be the loving mother of all, benign, patient, full of mercy and goodness toward the brethren who are separated from her. To mankind, oppressed by so many difficulties, the Church says, as Peter said to the poor who begged alms from him: "I have neither gold nor silver, but what I have I give you; in the name of Jesus Christ of Nazareth, rise and walk" (Acts 3:6). In other words, the Church does not offer to the men of today riches that pass, nor does she promise them a merely earthly happiness. But she distributes to them the goods of divine grace which, raising men to the dignity of sons of God, are the most efficacious safeguards and aids toward a more human life. She opens the fountain of her life-giving doctrine which allows men, enlightened by the light of Christ, to understand well what they really are, what their lofty dignity and their purpose are, and, finally through her children, she spreads everywhere the fullness of Christian charity, than which nothing is more effective in eradicating the seeds of discord, nothing more efficacious in promoting concord, just peace, and the brotherly unity of all. (*Pope John XXIII's opening speech to the Second Vatican Council, October 11, 1962*)
— *DV,* 713–14, 715, 715–17

These fruits that we expect so much from the Council, and on which we like so often to dwell, entail a vast program of work which is now being prepared. This concerns the doctrinal and practical problems which correspond more to the requirements of perfect conformity with Christian teaching, for the edification and in the service of the Mystical Body and of its supernatural mission, and, therefore, the sacred books, venerable tradition, the sacraments, prayer, ecclesiastical discipline, charitable and relief activities, the lay apostolate, and mission horizon.

The supernatural order must, however, reflect its efficiency in the other order, the temporal one, which on so many occasions is unfortunately ultimately the only one that occupies and worries man. In this field, the Church also has shown that it wishes to be *Mater et Magistra* — Mother and Teacher — according to the words of our distant and glorious predecessor, Innocent III, spoken on the occasion of the Fourth Lateran Council.

Though not having direct earthly ends, it cannot, however, in its mission fail to interest itself in the problems and worries of here below. It knows how beneficial to the good of the soul are those means that are apt to make the life of those individual men who must be saved more human. It knows that by vivifying the temporal order with the light of Christ it reveals men to themselves; it leads them, therefore, to discover in themselves their own nature, their own dignity, their own end.

Hence, the living presence of the Church extends, by right and by fact, to the international organizations, and to the working out of its social doctrine regarding the family, education, civil society, and all related problems. This has raised its magisterium to a very high level as the most authoritative voice, interpreter, and affirmer of the moral order, and champion of the rights and duties of all human beings and of all political communities.

In this way, the beneficial influence of the Council deliberations must, as we sincerely hope, succeed to the extent of imbuing with Christian light and penetrating with fervent spiritual energy not only the intimacy of the soul but the whole collection of human activities. (*Apostolic constitution "Humanae Salutis" in which Pope John XXIII convokes the Second Vatican Council, dated December 25, 1961*)   — *DV*, 706–7

Ecumenical Councils, whenever they are assembled, are a solemn celebration of the union of Christ and his Church, and hence lead to the universal radiation of truth, to the proper guidance of individuals in domestic and social life, to the strengthening of spiritual energies for a perennial uplift toward real and everlasting goodness.

The testimony of this extraordinary magisterium of the Church in the succeeding epochs of these twenty centuries of Christian history stands before us collected in numerous and imposing volumes, which are the sacred patrimony of our ecclesiastical archives, here in Rome and in the more noted libraries of the entire world....

Illuminated by the light of this Council, the Church — we confidently trust — will become greater in spiritual riches and, gaining the strength of new energies therefrom, she will look to the future without fear. In fact, by bringing herself up to date where required, and by the wise organization of mutual cooperation, the Church will make men, families, and peoples really turn their minds to heavenly things....

In the daily exercise of our pastoral office, we sometimes have to listen, much to our regret, to voices of persons who, though burning with zeal, are not endowed with too much sense of discretion or measure. In these modern times they can see nothing but prevarication and ruin. They say that our era, in comparison with past eras, is getting worse, and they behave as though they had learned nothing from history, which is, nonetheless, the teacher of life. They behave as though at the time of former Councils everything was a full triumph for the Christian idea and life and for proper religious liberty.

We feel we must disagree with those prophets of gloom, who are always forecasting disaster, as though the end of the world were at hand.

In the present order of things, divine providence is leading us to a new order of human relations which, by men's own efforts, and even beyond their very expectations, are directed toward the fulfillment of God's superior and inscrutable designs. And everything, even human differences, leads to the greater good of the Church.

It is easy to discern this reality if we consider attentively the world of today, which is so busy with politics and controversies in the economic order that it does not find time to attend to the care of spiritual reality, with which the Church's magisterium is concerned. Such a way of acting is certainly not right, and must justly be disapproved. It cannot be denied, however, that these new conditions of modern life have at least the advantage of having eliminated those innumerable obstacles by which, at one time, the sons of this world impeded the free action of the Church. In fact, it suffices to leaf even cursorily through the pages of ecclesiastical history to note clearly how the Ecumenical Councils themselves, while constituting a series of true glories for the Catholic Church, were often held to the accompaniment of most serious difficulties and sufferings because of the undue interference of civil authorities. The princes of this world, indeed, sometimes in all sincerity, intended thus to protect the Church. But more frequently this occurred not without spiritual damage and danger, since their interest therein was guided by the views of a selfish and perilous policy.

In this regard, we confess to you that we feel most poignant sorrow over the fact that very many bishops, so dear to us, are noticeable here today by their absence, because they are imprisoned for their faithfulness to Christ, or impeded by other restraints. The thought of them impels us to raise most fervent prayer to God. Nevertheless, we see today, not without great hopes and to our immense consolation, that the Church, finally freed from so many obstacles of a profane nature such as trammeled her in the past, can from this Vatican Basilica, as if from a second apostolic cenacle, and through your intermediary, raise her voice resonant, with majesty and greatness. (*Pope John XXIII's opening speech to the Second Vatican Council, October 11, 1962*) —*DV*, 711, 712, 712–13

Today the Church is witnessing a crisis under way within society. While humanity is on the edge of a new era, tasks of immense gravity and amplitude await the Church, as in the most tragic periods of its history. It is a question in fact of bringing the modern world into contact with the vivifying and perennial energies of the

Gospel, a world which exalts itself with its conquests in the technical and scientific fields, but which brings also the consequences of a temporal order which some have wished to reorganize excluding God. This is why modern society is earmarked by a great material progress to which there is not a corresponding advance in the moral field.

Hence there is a weakening in the aspiration toward the values of the spirit. Hence an urge for the almost exclusive search for earthly pleasures, which progressive technology places with such ease within the reach of all. And hence there is a completely new and disconcerting fact: the existence of a militant atheism which is active on a world level.

These painful considerations are a reminder of the duty to be vigilant and to keep the sense of responsibility awake. Distrustful souls see only darkness burdening the face of the earth. We, instead, like to reaffirm all our confidence in our Savior, who has not left the world which he redeemed. . . .

In the face of this twofold spectacle — a world which reveals a grave state of spiritual poverty and the Church of Christ, which is still so vibrant with vitality — we, from the time we ascended to the supreme pontificate, despite our unworthiness and by means of an impulse of divine providence, have felt immediately the urgency of the duty to call our sons together, to give the Church the possibility to contribute more efficaciously to the solution of the problems of the modern age.

For this reason, welcoming as from above the intimate voice of our spirit, we considered that the times now were right to offer to the Catholic Church and to the world the gift of a new Ecumenical Council, as an addition to, and continuation of, the series of the twenty great councils, which have been through the centuries a truly heavenly providence for the increase of grace and Christian progress. (*Apostolic constitution "Humanae Salutis" in which Pope John XXIII convokes the Second Vatican Council, dated December 25, 1961)*   — *DV,* 703–4, 705

TOWARD UNITY

Now we shall discuss a unity which is of particular concern to Us and is closely connected to the pastoral mission which God has entrusted to Us: the unity of the Church.   — *APC*, 59

One Fold and One Shepherd

Everyone realizes, of course, that God our Redeemer founded this society which was to endure to the end of time, for as Christ said, "Behold, I am with you all days, even unto the consummation of the world" (Matt. 28:20). For this intention he addressed ardent prayers to his Father: "That all may be one, even as thou, Father, in me and I in thee; that they also may be one in Us" (John 17:21). Surely this prayer was heard and granted because of his reverent submission (see Heb. 5:7). This is a comforting hope; it assures us that someday all the sheep who are not of this fold will want to return to it. Then, in the words of God our Savior, "there shall be one fold and one shepherd" (John 10:16).   — *APC*, 60

An Ecumenical Council

This fond hope compelled Us to make public Our intention to hold an Ecumenical Council. Bishops from every part of the world will gather there to discuss serious religious topics. They will consider, in particular, the growth of the Catholic faith, the restoration of sound morals among the Christian flock, and appropriate adaptation of Church discipline to the needs and conditions of our times.

This event will be a wonderful spectacle of truth, unity, and charity. For those who behold it but are not one with this Apostolic See, We hope that it will be a gentle invitation to seek and find that unity for which Jesus Christ prayed so ardently to his Father in heaven.   — *APC*, 61–62

Movements toward Union

We are already aware, to Our great joy, that many of the communities that are separated from the See of Blessed Peter have recently shown some inclination toward the Catholic faith and its teachings. They have manifested a high regard for this Apostolic See and an esteem which grows greater from day to day as devotion to truth overcomes earlier misconceptions.

We have taken note that almost all those who are adorned with the name of Christian even though separated from Us and from one another have sought to forge bonds of unity by means of many congresses and by establishing councils. This is evidence that they are moved by an intense desire for unity of some kind.   — *APC, 63–64*

A Mark of Christ's Church

When the divine Redeemer founded his Church, there is no doubt that he made firm unity its cornerstone and one of its essential attributes. Had he not done this — and it is absurd even to make such a suggestion — he would have founded a transient thing, which in time, at least, would destroy itself. For in just this way have nearly all philosophies risen from among the vagaries of human opinion: one after another, they come into being, they evolve, they are forgotten. But this clearly cannot be the history of a divine teaching authority founded by Jesus Christ, "the way, the truth, and the life" (John 14:6).

But this unity, Venerable Brethren and beloved sons, must be solid, firm and sure, not transient, uncertain, or unstable. Though there is no such unity in other Christian communities, all who look carefully can see that it is present in the Catholic Church.   — *APC, 65–66*

Three Unities

Indeed, the Catholic Church is set apart and distinguished by these three characteristics: unity of doctrine, unity of organization, unity of worship. This unity is so conspicuous that by it all men can find and recognize the Catholic Church.

It is the will of God, the Church's founder, that all the sheep should eventually gather into this one fold, under the guidance of one shepherd. All God's children are summoned to their father's only home, and its cornerstone is Peter. All men should work together like brothers to become part of this single kingdom of God; for the citizens of that kingdom are united in peace and harmony on earth that they might enjoy eternal happiness some day in heaven. —APC, 67–68

Unity of Doctrine

The Catholic Church teaches the necessity of believing firmly and faithfully all that God has revealed. This revelation is contained in sacred scripture and in the oral and written tradition that has come down through the centuries from the apostolic age and finds expression in the ordinances and definitions of the popes and legitimate Ecumenical Councils.

Whenever a man has wandered from this path, the Church has never failed to use her maternal authority to call him again and again to the right road. She knows well that there is no other truth than the one truth she treasures; that there can be no "truths" in contradiction of it. Thus she repeats and bears witness to the words of the Apostle: "For we can do nothing against the truth, but only for the truth" (2 Cor. 13:8). —APC, 69–70

Religious Controversy

The Catholic Church, of course, leaves many questions open to the discussion of theologians. She does this to the extent that matters are not absolutely certain. Far from jeopardizing the Church's unity, controversies, as a noted English author, Cardinal John Henry Newman, has remarked, can actually pave the way for its attainment. For discussion can lead to fuller and deeper understanding of religious truths; when one idea strikes against another, there may be a spark.

But the common saying, expressed in various ways and attributed to various authors, must be recalled with approval: in essentials, unity; in doubtful matters, liberty; in all things, charity.   — APC, 71–72

Unity in Organization

That there is unity in the administration of the Catholic Church is evident. For as the faithful are subject to their priests, so are priests to their bishops, whom "the Holy Spirit has placed . . . to rule the Church of God" (Acts 20:28). So, too, every bishop is subject to the Roman pontiff, the successor of Saint Peter, whom Christ called a rock and made the foundation of his Church (see Matt. 16:18). It was to Peter that Christ gave in a special way the power to bind and loose on earth (see Matt. 16:19), to strengthen his brethren (see Luke 22:32), to feed the entire flock (see John 21:15–17).   — APC, 73

Unity of Worship

As for unity of worship, the Catholic Church has had seven sacraments, neither more nor less, from her beginning right down to the present day. Jesus Christ left her these sacraments as a sacred legacy, and she has never ceased to administer them throughout the Catholic world and thus to feed and foster the supernatural life of the faithful.   — APC, 74

THE SECOND VATICAN COUNCIL AND UNITY

Venerable Brethren, the time is drawing near for the Second General Council of the Vatican. Surrounding the Roman pontiff and in close communion with him, you, the bishops, will present to the world a wonderful spectacle of Catholic unity. Meanwhile We, for Our part, will seek to give instruction and comfort by briefly recalling to mind St. Leo's high ideals regarding the Church's unity. Our intention in so doing is indeed to honor the memory of a most wise pope, but at the same time to give the faithful profitable food for thought on the eve of this great event.   — *ADS*, 35

A CALL TO UNITY

Our purpose, Venerable Brethren, in focusing attention on these facts has been to establish beyond doubt that in ancient times East and West alike were united in the generosity of their tribute to the holiness of St. Leo the Great. Would that it were so today; that those who are separated from the Church of Rome yet still have the welfare of the Church at heart, might bear witness once more to that ancient, universal esteem for St. Leo.

For if only they will settle their differences — those lamentable differences concerning the teaching and pastoral activity of this great pope — then the faith in which they believe will shine forth with renewed splendor; namely, that "there is one God, and one mediator of God and men, the man Christ Jesus" (1 Tim. 2:5).   — *ADS*, 59–60

Universality of Christ's Command

We are St. Leo's successor in Peter's See of Rome. We share in Peter's See of Rome. We share his firm belief in the divine origin of that command which Jesus Christ gave to the apostles and their successors to preach the Gospel and bring eternal salvation

to the whole world. We cherish, therefore, St. Leo's desire to see
all men enter the way of truth, charity, and peace. — *ADS,* 61

The Council

It is to render the Church better able to fulfill this high mission
of hers that We have resolved to summon the Second General
Council of the Vatican. We are fully confident that this solemn
assembly of the Catholic hierarchy will not only reinforce that
unity in faith, worship and discipline which is a distinguishing
mark of Christ's true Church, but will also attract the gaze of the
great majority of Christians of every denomination, and induce
them to gather around "the great Pastor of the sheep" (Heb.
13:20) who entrusted his flock to the unfailing guardianship of
Peter and his successors (see John 21:15–17).   — *ADS,* 62

That All May Be One

But out greatest desire is that this Our call to unity shall re-echo
the Savior's prayer to his Father at the Last Supper: "That they
all may be one, as thou, Father, in me, and I in thee; that they
also may be one in Us" (John 17:21).

Are we to say that this prayer went unheeded by the heavenly
Father, who yet accepted the sacrifice of Christ's blood on the
Cross? Did not Christ say that his Father never failed to hear
him? (See John 11:42.) He prayed for the Church; he sacrificed
himself on the Cross for it, and promised it his unfailing presence.
Assuredly, then, we must believe that this Church has always
been, and still is, one, holy, catholic and apostolic; for thus was
it founded.   — *ADS,* 65–66

Some Hopeful Signs

Unfortunately, however, the sort of unity whereby all believers
in Christ profess the same faith, practice the same worship, and

obey the same supreme authority is no more evident among the Christians of today than it was in bygone ages. We do, however, see more and more men of good will in various parts of the world earnestly striving to bring about this visible unity among Christians, a unity which truly accords with the divine Savior's intentions, commands, and desires; and this to Us is a source of joyous consolation and ineffable hope. This desire for unity, We know, is fostered in them by the Holy Spirit, and it can only be realized in the way in which Jesus Christ has prophesied it: "There will be one fold and one shepherd" (John 10:16). — *ADS*, 67

Day of Peace and Reconciliation

We therefore beg and implore Christ Our Mediator and Advocate with the Father (see 1 Tim. 2:5; 1 John 2:1) to give all Christians the grace to recognize those marks by which his true Church is distinguished from all others, and to become its devoted sons. May God in his infinite kindness hasten the dawn of that long-awaited day of joyful, universal reconciliation. Then will all Christ's redeemed, united in a single family, join in praising the divine Mercy, singing in joyous harmony those words of the psalmist of old: "Behold, how good and how pleasant it is for brethren to dwell together in unity" (Ps. 132:1). — *ADS*, 68

The Church's solicitude to promote and defend truth derives from the fact that, according to the plan of God, who wills all men to be saved and to come to the knowledge of the truth (1 Tim. 2:4), men without the assistance of the whole of revealed doctrine cannot reach a complete and firm unity of minds, with which are associated true peace and eternal salvation.

Unfortunately, the entire Christian family has not yet fully attained this visible unity in truth.

The Catholic Church, therefore, considers it her duty to work actively so that there may be fulfilled the great mystery of that unity, which Jesus Christ invoked with fervent prayer from his heavenly Father on the eve of his sacrifice. She rejoices in peace, knowing well that she is intimately associated with that prayer, and then exults greatly at seeing that invocation extend its efficacy with salutary fruit, even among those who are outside her fold.

Indeed, if one considers well this same unity which Christ implored for his Church, it seems to shine, as it were, with a triple ray of beneficent supernal light: namely, the unity of Catholics among themselves, which must always be kept exemplary and most firm; the unity of prayers and ardent desires with which those Christians separated from this Apostolic See aspire to be united with us; and the unity in esteem and respect for the Catholic Church which animates those who follow non-Christian religions.

In this regard, it is a source of considerable sorrow to see that the greater part of the human race — although all men who are born were redeemed by the blood of Christ — does not yet participate in those sources of divine grace which exist in the Catholic Church. Hence the Church, whose light illuminates all, whose strength of supernatural unity redounds to the advantage of all humanity, is rightly described in these beautiful words of St. Cyprian: "The Church, surrounded by divine light, spreads her rays over the entire earth. This light, however, is one and unique, and shines everywhere without causing any separation in the unity of the body. She extends her branches over the whole world. By her fruitfulness she sends ever farther afield her rivulets. Nevertheless, the head is always one, the origin one, for she is the one mother, abundantly fruitful. We are born of her, are nourished by her milk, we live of her spirit." (Pope John XXIII's *Opening speech to the Second Vatican Council,* October 11, 1962)

— *DV,* 717–18

Respect for the Opinions of Others

Beware of misunderstandings: they arise, challenge each other, and come to blows. We must be on our guard against them; if they cannot be avoided, at least let us not cultivate them, or allow them to be exaggerated in our imagination. Let us try, unashamedly, to be the first to explain them away, to put things right once more, to disentangle them, and to keep ourselves free from any feeling of resentment.

Even among cultured and spiritual people there may be a variety of opinions and views in matters open to discussion. This does no harm to charity and peace, as long as we preserve moderation of manner and harmony of minds. I will add moreover that the Lord makes use of these misunderstandings to bring about in other ways some great good. Thus Paul and Barnabas separated because of young John Mark . . . and yet they were both equally righteous and holy. With souls like these everything is set right by the Lord's grace. But this does not alter the fact that we must beware of misunderstandings and must try to clear them away.

We can never forget those words of our Lord's which so surprised the world, when he said that it gives more joy and peace to the heart to believe and to renounce than to demand and receive.

— *PD, 139*

An Invitation to Union

We address Ourselves now to all of you who are separated from this Apostolic See. May this wonderful Spectacle of unity, by which the Catholic Church is set apart and distinguished, as well as the prayers and entreaties with which she begs God for unity, stir your hearts and awaken you to what is really in your best interest.

May We, in fond anticipation, address you as sons and brethren? May We hope with a father's love for your return?

Once when a terrible schism was rending the seamless garment of the Church, Bishop Theophilus of Alexandria addressed his sons and brethren with words of pastoral zeal. We take pleasure in addressing these same words to you: "Dearly beloved, we have all been invited to heaven. Let each, then, according to his abilities imitate Jesus, our model and the author of our salvation.

"Let us embrace that humility of soul which elevates us to great heights, that charity which unites us with God; let us have a genuine faith in revealed mysteries.

"Avoid division, shun discord, . . . encourage charity toward one another. Heed the words of Christ: 'By this will all men know that you are my disciples, if you have love for one another.' "

When We fondly call you to the unity of the Church, please observe that We are not inviting you to a strange home, but to your own, to the abode of your forefathers. Permit Us, then, to long for you all "in the heart of Christ Jesus" (Phil. 1:8), and to exhort you all to be mindful of your forefathers who "preached God's word to you; contemplate the happy issue of the life they lived, and imitate their faith" (Heb. 13:7).

There is in paradise a glorious legion of Saints who have passed to heaven from your people. By the example of their lives they seem to summon you to union with this Apostolic See with which your Christian community was beneficially united for so many centuries. You are summoned especially by those Saints who in their writings perpetuated and explained with admirable accuracy the teachings of Jesus Christ.

We address, then, as brethren all who are separated from Us, using the words of Saint Augustine: "Whether they wish it or not, they are our brethren. They cease to be our brethren only when they stop saying 'Our Father.' "

"Let us love God our Lord; let us love his Church. Let us love him as our father and her as our mother, him as our master and her as his handmaid. For we are the children of his handmaid. This marriage is based on a deep love. No one can offend one of them and be a friend of the other. . . . What difference does it make that you have not offended your father, if he punishes offenses against your mother? . . . Therefore, dearly beloved, be all of one mind and remain true to God your father and your mother the Church."   — *APC*, 79–87

CHRISTIAN PARTICIPATION

Lay Apostolate's Role in Social Education

The Lay Apostolate, therefore, has an important role to play in social education — especially those associations and organizations which have as their specific objective the Christianization of contemporary society. The members of these associations, besides profiting personally from their own day-to-day experience in this field, can also help in the social education of the rising generation by giving it the benefit of the experience they have gained.   — MM, 233

Christian Spirit — Not Hedonism

But We must remind you here of an important truth: the Christian conception of life demands of all — whether highborn or lowly — a spirit of moderation and sacrifice. That is what God calls us to by his grace.

There is, alas, a spirit of hedonism abroad today which beguiles men into thinking that life is nothing more than the quest for pleasure and the satisfaction of human passions. This attitude is disastrous. Its evil effects on soul and body are undeniable. Even on the natural level temperance and simplicity of life are the dictates of sound policy. On the supernatural level, the Gospels and the whole ascetic tradition of the Church require a sense of mortification and penance which assures the rule of the spirit over the flesh, and offers an efficacious means of expiating the punishment due to sin, from which no one, except Jesus Christ and his Immaculate Mother, is exempt.   — MM, 234–35

Practical Suggestions

There are three stages which should normally be followed in the reduction of social principles into practice. First, one reviews the concrete situation; secondly, one forms a judgment on it in the light of these same principles; thirdly, one decides what in the circumstances can and should be done to implement these principles. These are the three stages that are usually expressed in the three terms: look, judge, act.

It is important for our young people to grasp this method and to practice it. Knowledge acquired in this way does not remain merely abstract, but is seen as something that must be translated into action.   — *MM,* 236–37

When Differences Arise . . .

Differences of opinion in the application of principles can sometimes arise even among sincere Catholics. When this happens, they should be careful not to lose their respect and esteem for each other. Instead, they should strive to find points of agreement for effective and suitable action, and not wear themselves out in interminable arguments and, under pretext of the better or the best, omit to do the good that is possible and therefore obligatory.

In their economic and social activities, Catholics often come into contact with others who do not share their view of life. In such circumstances, they must, of course, bear themselves as Catholics and do nothing to compromise religion and morality. Yet at the same time they should show themselves animated by a spirit of understanding and unselfishness, ready to cooperate loyally in achieving objects which are good in themselves, or can be turned to good. Needless to say, when the hierarchy has made a decision on any point Catholics are bound to obey their directives. The Church has the right and obligation not merely to guard ethical and religious principles, but also to declare its authoritative judgment in the matter of putting these principles into practice.   — *MM,* 238–39

The Layman's Responsibility

These, then, are the educational principles which must be put into effect. It is a task which belongs particularly to Our sons, the laity, for it is their lot to live an active life in the world and organize themselves for the attainment of temporal ends.

In performing this task, which is a noble one, they must not only be well qualified in their trade or profession and practice it in accordance with its own proper laws; they must also bring their professional activity into conformity with the Church's social teaching. Their attitude must be one of loyal trust and filial obedience to ecclesiastical authority.

They must remember, too, that if in the transaction of their temporal affairs they take no account of those social principles which the Church teaches, and which We now confirm, then they fail in their obligations and may easily violate the rights of others. They may even go so far as to bring discredit on the Church's teaching, lending substance to the opinion that, in spite of its intrinsic value, it is in fact powerless to direct men's lives. — *MM, 240–41*

The Christian's Work in the World

We have only been able to touch lightly upon this matter, but Our sons, the laity especially, must not suppose that they would be acting prudently to lessen their personal Christian commitment in this passing world. On the contrary, We insist that they must intensify it and increase it continually.

In his solemn prayer for the Church's unity, Christ Our Lord did not ask his Father to remove his disciples from the world: "I pray not that thou shouldst take them out of the world, but that thou shouldst keep them from evil" (John 17:15). Let no man therefore imagine that a life of activity in the world is incompatible with spiritual perfection. The two can very well be harmonized. It is a gross error to suppose that a man cannot perfect himself except by putting aside all temporal activity, on the plea that such activity

will inevitably lead him to compromise his personal dignity as a
human being and as a Christian.   — *MM, 254–55*

Perfection through Daily Work

That a man should develop and perfect himself through his daily
work — which in most cases is of a temporal character — is
perfectly in keeping with the plan of divine providence. The
Church today is faced with an immense task: to humanize and
to Christianize this modern civilization of ours. The continued
development of this civilization, indeed its very survival, demand
and insist that the Church do her part in the world. That is why,
as We said before, she claims the cooperation of her laity. In con-
ducting their human affairs to the best of their ability, they must
recognize that they are doing a service to humanity, in intimate
union with God through Christ, and to God's greater glory. And
St. Paul insisted: "Whether you eat or drink, or whatsoever else
you do, do all to the glory of God" (1 Cor. 10:31). "All whatsoever you do in word or in work, do all in the name of the
Lord Jesus Christ, giving thanks to God and the Father by him"
(Col. 3:17).   — *MM, 256*

Greater Efficiency in Temporal Affairs

To search for spiritual perfection and eternal salvation in the
conduct of human affairs and institutions is not to rob these
of the power to achieve their immediate, specific ends, but to
enhance this power.

The words of our divine Master are true for all time: "Seek
ye therefore first the kingdom of God and his justice; and all
these things shall be added unto you" (Matt. 6:33). The man
who is "light in the Lord" (Eph. 5:8) and who walks as a "child
of the light" (see ibid.) has a sure grasp of the fundamental demands of justice in all life's difficulties and complexities, obscured

though they may be by so much individual, national, and racial selfishness.

Animated, too, by the charity of Christ, he finds it impossible not to love his fellow men. He makes his own their needs, their sufferings, and their joys. There is a sureness of touch in all his activity in every field. It is energetic, generous, and considerate. For "charity is patient, is kind; charity envieth not, dealeth not perversely, is not puffed up, is not ambitious, seeketh not her own, is not provoked to anger, thinketh no evil; rejoiceth not in iniquity, but rejoiceth with the truth; beareth all things, believeth all things, hopeth all things, endureth all things" (1 Cor. 13:4–7). — *MM*, 257

Here once more We exhort Our sons to take an active part in public life, and to work together for the benefit of the whole human race, as well as for their own political communities. It is vitally necessary for them to endeavor, in the light of Christian faith, and with love as their guide, to ensure that every institution, whether economic, social, cultural or political, be such as not to obstruct but rather to facilitate man's self betterment, both in the natural and in the supernatural order. — *PT*, 146

Scientific Competence, Technical Capacity, and Professional Experience

And yet, if they are to imbue civilization with right ideals and Christian principles, it is not enough for Our sons to be illumined by the heavenly light of faith and to be fired with enthusiasm for a cause; they must involve themselves in the work of these institutions and strive to influence them effectively from within.

But in a culture and civilization like our own, which is so remarkable for its scientific knowledge and its technical discoveries, clearly no one can insinuate himself into public life unless he be scientifically competent, technically capable, and skilled in the practice of his own profession. — *PT*, 147–48

Apostolate of a Trained Laity

And yet even this must be reckoned insufficient to bring the relationships of daily life into conformity with a more human standard, based, as it must be, on truth, tempered by justice, motivated by mutual love, and holding fast to the practice of freedom.

If these policies are really to become operative, men must first of all take the utmost care to conduct their various temporal activities in accordance with the laws which govern each and every such activity, observing the principles which correspond to their respective natures. Secondly, men's actions must be made to conform with the precepts of the moral order. This means that their behavior must be such as to reflect their consciousness of exercising a personal right or performing a personal duty. Reason has a further demand to make. In obedience to the providential designs and commands of God respecting our salvation and neglecting the dictates of conscience, men must conduct themselves in their temporal activity in such a way as to effect a thorough integration of the principal spiritual values with those of science, technology, and the professions.   — PT, 149–50

Constant Endeavor

In this connection We think it opportune to point out how difficult it is to understand clearly the relation between the objective requirements of justice and concrete situations; to define, that is, correctly to what degree and in what form doctrinal principles and directives must be applied in the given state of human society.

The definition of these degrees and forms is all the more difficult in an age such as ours, driven forward by a fever of activity. And yet this is the age in which each one of us is required to make his own contribution to the universal common good. Daily is borne in on us the need to make the reality of social life conform better to the requirements of justice. Hence Our sons have every reason for not thinking that they can relax their efforts and be satisfied with what they have already achieved.

What has so far been achieved is insufficient compared with what needs to be done; all men must realize that. Every day provides a more important, a more fitting enterprise to which they must turn their hands — industry, trade unions, professional organizations, insurance, cultural institutions, the law, politics, medical and recreational facilities, and other such activities. The age in which we live needs all these things. It is an age in which men, having discovered the atom and achieved the breakthrough into outer space, are now exploring other avenues, leading to almost limitless horizons.   — *PT,* 154–56

Relations between Catholics and Non-Catholics in Social and Economic Affairs

The principles We have set out in this document take their rise from the very nature of things. They derive, for the most part, from the consideration of man's natural rights. Thus the putting of these principles into effect frequently involves extensive cooperation between Catholics and those Christians who are separated from this Apostolic See. It even involves the cooperation of Catholics with men who may not be Christians but who nevertheless are reasonable men, and men of natural moral integrity. "In such circumstances they must, of course, bear themselves as Catholics, and do nothing to compromise religion and morality. Yet at the same time they should show themselves animated by a spirit of understanding and unselfishness, ready to cooperate loyally in achieving objects which are good in themselves, or conducive to good [MM 239]."   — *PT,* 157

The Christian faithful, members of a living organism, cannot remain aloof and think that they have done their duty when they have satisfied their own spiritual needs; every individual must give his assistance to those who are working for the increase

and propagation of God's kingdom. Our predecessor Pius XII
reminded all of their common duty in these words: "A principal
note of the Church is catholicity; consequently, a man is no true
member of the Church unless he is likewise a true member of
the entire body of Christian believers and is filled with an ardent
desire to see her take root and flourish in every land." — *PP*, 40

Christians in Public Life

The laymen of mission countries exert their most direct and effective influence in the field of public activity, and it is necessary
that Christian communities take urgent, timely measures to bring
laymen into the public life of their countries for the common
good — men who not only acquit themselves creditably in their
professions and trades, but are also an asset to the Church which
re-created them in her grace. Thus may their pastors praise them
with the words which we read in the writings of St. Basil: "I
thanked the Most Holy God for the fact that, even though busily
attending to public affairs, you did not neglect the interests of the
Church: on the contrary, each one of you has been solicitous of
her affairs just as though they had been your own private affairs
and, indeed, as though your life depended on it."

Particularly in the field of education, in organized public welfare, in trade unions, and in public administration, will the talents
of local Catholic experts play a paramount role, if they, following
the duty imposed by their consciences — a duty whose neglect
would be traitorous — base their thinking and action on Christian principles. These, as we learn from experience acquired in the
course of many centuries, possess the highest power and influence
for the pursuit of the common good.   — *PP*, 49–50

Aid to Missions from Catholic Groups

Everybody knows how the mutual assistance which is exchanged
among Catholic organizations established all over the world can

be — as Our predecessor Pius XII has pointed out — of great use and much value to the apostolate of the laity in mission territories. On the educational plane, these organizations can help by devising Christian solutions to current problems, especially social problems, in the newly established nations; on the apostolic plane, they can help by recruiting and organizing a body of laymen, willing to serve under Christ's banner. We know that this has been done, and is being done, by lay missionaries who chose to leave their countries, either temporarily or for life, in order to contribute, by manifold activities, to the social and religious welfare of mission countries. Let us pray fervently to God that the numbers of these generous Christians be multiplied, and that God's support will never be absent in their difficulties and labors, which they are meeting with truly apostolic spirit. The secular institutes will be able to give the local laity in mission territories generous and loyal help, if, by their example, they attract imitators, and if they place their talents and work, promptly and willingly, at the disposal of the local ordinaries, in order to speed the growing-up process of the new Christian communities.

— PP, 51

Lay Help from Afar

We appeal especially to all Catholic laymen everywhere who are distinguishing themselves in their professions and in public life to consider seriously how they can help their newly acquired brethren in the Faith, even without leaving their countries. They can do this by giving them the benefit of their advice, their experience, and their technical assistance; they can, without too much labor or grave inconvenience, sometimes give them help that will be decisive. Good men will surely find a way to fulfill this fatherly desire of Ours. They will make Our wish known to those whom they find favorably disposed, in order first to arouse good will, and then to channel it into the most suitable work.   *— PP, 52*

Christian Charity

Charity is the summit of human and Christian virtue...at the point of union between earth and heaven, which is sublimely expressed in Christ Jesus, the Word of the Father, who became man to save mankind. The Creator of the world, in order to save fallen man, took on a human body and "made us partakers in his divine nature" (see 2 Pet. 1:4).

These are moving and mysterious words, enshrining in celestial light the doctrine of the redemption of the world and of the divine institution of Christ's Church.

In this holy Church we have all received, and continue to receive, life from Jesus who, by becoming our Brother, has laid the foundation of the great precept of neighborly charity, of which the Savior said, foretelling the terms of the Last Judgment: "As you did it to one of the least of these my brethren, the poor, the abandoned and the needy, you did it to me" (see Matt. 25:40).

These words demand a corresponding charity from all Christians as if by way of repaying Jesus himself for making us "partakers of his divine nature."

Oh how wonderful is the story of Christian charity, which continues to shine through all the centuries!   — PD, 162

Our Duty to Our Neighbor

Justice is an admirable virtue. We hear it much spoken of and yet, in our daily lives, we live in the midst of great injustices, due to the manner in which so many people behave and act. The first flagrant injustice is apparent all around us. We have only to reflect on the huge number of people who take not the slightest interest in spiritual things, in all that reflects the Gospel message, dedicating themselves exclusively to profit-making, the pursuit of pleasure, and the satisfaction of their own selfish desires.

When we have firm principles of right judgment and justice, we can make good and swift progress in God's company. Our duty is not to remain inert, but to lead active lives that do honor to our principles.

If you have a family, try to be worthy of this mission and responsibility. If you have uncommon talents or gifts that you can use in higher spheres of educational or artistic activity, you must employ these talents for the purposes assigned by God's law. If you are rich in resources and material possessions, your first duty is to remember that whatever you do not need and have left over, you must, according to the noble Gospel doctrine, give to others who need your help.

We are dismayed when we read or hear about some aspects of modern life. Notwithstanding all that is done and said and organized, and all the progress made in scientific techniques and communications, there are still today millions of undernourished human beings, many of whom die of starvation. They die deprived of what they have a right to claim, for God created the heavens and the earth to satisfy the basic needs of life.   — *PD,* 188–89

The Christian's Duty in the World

It would be wrong for our children, and especially for the laity, to consider that prudence required a slackening of Christian activity in the world; on the contrary, they must renew and increase it.

The Lord, in his sublime prayer for the unity of his Church, did not implore his Father to remove his followers from the world, but to preserve them from evil. We must not create an artificial opposition where it does not exist, that is, between our own endeavor to sanctify ourselves and our active presence in the life of the world around us; it is not true, either that personal salvation can be found only in temporal activities, or that such activities fatally compromise the dignity of human beings, and particularly of believers.

Instead, it is perfectly in accordance with the design of providence that everyone should try to save his own soul through his daily work, which is for nearly all human beings work for a merely temporal purpose.

Our lay children must feel it is their duty to fulfill their professional obligations, as they are in honor bound to do, for this is a service to society, but at the same time to remain in spiritual communion with God and in Christ, working for his glory, as the Apostle Paul says: "So whether you eat or drink, or whatever you do, do all to the glory of God" (1 Cor. 10:31). — *PD*, 197

4

Seeds for a New World Order

The new world order, in truth, is not the new geo-political order that occurs according to the dreams or moods of the mightiest, the wealthiest, or the most cunning. The essence of the new world order is in "the diligent observance of the divinely established order" (PT, introduction), and revealed in the Gospel message: love, peace, justice, and brotherhood. Such a message makes possible to define, without biases and distortions, a true social order based on rights, duties, responsibilities, and genuine cooperation. Pope John XXIII proved to truly be a "genius for human relationships" (IT, 60), as he was described. Human rights, the common good, and especially peace were very dear to his heart and became major topics and works of his pontificate. Moreover, it is good to remember that Pope John was a military chaplain during World War I, and he knew firsthand—not conceptually, but experientially—the atrocities of wars. No wonder he could say in 1959, "War has always been, and still is, a very grave evil; and whoever is familiar with the mind of Christ and his Gospel, and has the spirit of human and Christian brotherhood, can never sufficiently detest it" (PD, 96–97). A new world order is urgently needed. Indeed.

BROTHERHOOD AND COOPERATION

The Brotherhood of Man

God created men as brothers, not foes. He gave them the earth to be cultivated by their toil and labor. Each and every man is to enjoy the fruits of the earth and receive from it his sustenance and the necessities of life. The various nations are simply communities of men, that is, of brothers. They are to work in brotherly cooperation for the common prosperity of human society, not simply for their own particular goals.   — APC, 23

A Journey to Immortal Life

Besides this, our journey through this mortal life should not be regarded as an end in itself, entered upon merely for pleasure. This journey leads beyond the burial of our human flesh to immortal life, to a fatherland which will endure forever.

If this teaching, this consoling hope, were taken away from men, there would be no reason for living. Lusts, dissensions, and disputes would erupt from within us. There would be no reasonable check to restrain them. The olive branch of peace would not shine in our thoughts; the firebrands of war would blaze there. Our lot would be cast with beasts, who do not have the use of reason. Ours would be an even worse lot, for we do have the use of reason and by abusing it (which, unfortunately, often happens) we can sink into a state lower than that of beasts. Like Cain, we would commit a terrible crime and stain the earth with our brother's blood.

Before all else, then, we must turn our thoughts to sound principles if we wish, as we should, to guide our actions along the path of justice.

We are called brothers. We actually are brothers. We share a common destiny in this life and the next. Why, then, do we act as though we are foes and enemies? Why do we envy one another?

Why do we stir up hatred? Why do we ready lethal weapons for use against our brothers?

There has already been enough warfare among men! Too many youths in the flower of life have shed their blood already! Legions of the dead, all fallen in battle, dwell within this earth of ours. Their stern voices urge us all to return at once to harmony, unity, and a just peace.

All men, then, should turn their attention away from those things that divide and separate us and should consider how they may be joined in mutual and just regard for one another's opinions and possessions.   — *APC*, 24–29

Obligation of the Wealthy Nations

Probably the most difficult problem today concerns the relationship between political communities that are economically advanced and those in the process of development. Whereas the standard of living is high in the former, the latter are subject to extreme poverty. The solidarity which binds all men together as members of a common family makes it impossible for wealthy nations to look with indifference upon the hunger, misery, and poverty of other nations whose citizens are unable to enjoy even elementary human rights. The nations of the world are becoming more and more dependent on one another and it will not be possible to preserve a lasting peace so long as glaring economic and social imbalances persist.

Mindful of Our position as the father of all peoples, We feel constrained to repeat here what We said on another occasion: "We are all equally responsible for the undernourished peoples. [Hence], it is necessary to educate one's conscience to the sense of responsibility which weighs upon each and every one, especially upon those who are more blessed with this world's goods."   — *MM*, 157–58

The Mystical Body of Christ

The Church has always emphasized that this obligation of helping those who are in misery and want should be felt most strongly by Catholics, in view of the fact that they are members of the Mystical Body of Christ. "In this we have known the charity of God," says St. John, "because he has laid down his life for us; and we ought to lay down our lives for the brethren. He that hath the substance of this world and shall see his brother in need and shall shut up his bowels from him; how doth the charity of God abide in him?" (1 John 3:16–17).

It is therefore a great source of joy to Us to see those nations which enjoy a high degree of economic wealth helping the nations not so well provided, so that they may more effectively raise their standard of living.   — MM, 159–60

International Aid

Justice and humanity demand that those countries which produce consumer goods, especially farm products, in excess of their own needs should come to the assistance of those other countries where large sections of the population are suffering from want and hunger. It is nothing less than an outrage to justice and humanity to destroy or to squander goods that other people need for their very lives.

We are, of course, well aware that overproduction, especially in agriculture, can cause economic harm to a certain section of the population. But it does not follow that one is thereby exonerated from extending emergency aid to those who need it. On the contrary, everything must be done to minimize the ill effects of overproduction and to spread the burden equitably over the entire population.   — MM, 161–62

Scientific, Technical, and Financial Co-operation

Of itself, however, emergency aid will not go far in relieving want and famine when these are caused — as they so often are — by the primitive state of a nation's economy. The only permanent remedy for this is to make use of every possible means of providing these citizens with the scientific, technical, and professional training they need, and to put at their disposal the necessary capital for speeding up their economic development with the help of modern methods.

We are aware how deeply the public conscience has been affected in recent years by the urgent need of supporting the economic development and social progress of those countries which are still struggling against poverty and economic disabilities.

International and regional organizations, national and private societies, all are working toward this goal, increasing day to day the measure of their own technical cooperation in all productive spheres. By their combined efforts thousands of young people are being given facilities for attending the universities of the more advanced countries and acquiring an up-to-date scientific, technical, and professional training. World banking institutes, individual states, and private persons are helping to furnish the capital for an ever richer network of economic enterprises in the less wealthy countries. It is a magnificent work that they are doing, and We are most happy to take this occasion of giving it the praise that it deserves. It is a work, however, which needs to be increased, and We hope that the years ahead will see the wealthier nations making even greater efforts for the scientific, technical, and economic advancement of those political communities whose development is still only in its initial stages.   — *MM*, 163–65

RIGHTS AND DUTIES

Rights

First We must speak of man's rights. Man has the right to live. He has the right to bodily integrity and to the means necessary for the proper development of life, particularly food, clothing, shelter, medical care, rest, and, finally, the necessary social services. In consequence, he has the right to be looked after in the event of ill health; disability stemming from his work; widowhood; old age; enforced unemployment; or whenever through no fault of his own he is deprived of the means of livelihood.   — *PT,* 11

Rights Pertaining to Moral and Cultural Values

Moreover, man has a natural right to be respected. He has a right to his good name. He has a right to freedom in investigating the truth, and — within the limits of the moral order and the common good — to freedom of speech and publication, and to freedom to pursue whatever profession he may choose. He has the right, also, to be accurately informed about public events.

He has the natural right to share in the benefits of culture, and hence to receive a good general education and a technical or professional training consistent with the degree of educational development in his own country. Furthermore, a system must be devised for affording gifted members of society the opportunity of engaging in more advanced studies, with a view to their occupying, as far as possible, positions of responsibility in society in keeping with their natural talent and acquired skill. — *PT,* 12–13

The Right to Worship God according to One's Conscience

Also among man's rights is that of being able to worship God in accordance with the right dictates of his own conscience, and to profess his religion both in private and in public. According to the clear teaching of Lactantius, "This is the very condition of our birth, that we render to the God who made us that just homage which is his due; that we acknowledge him alone as God, and follow him. It is from this ligature of piety, which binds us and joins us to God, that religion derives its name."

Hence, too, Pope Leo XIII declared that "true freedom, freedom worthy of the sons of God, is that freedom which most truly safeguards the dignity of the human person. It is stronger than any violence or injustice. Such is the freedom which has always been desired by the Church, and which she holds most dear. It is the sort of freedom which the Apostles resolutely claimed for themselves. The apologists defended it in their writings; thousands of martyrs consecrated it with their blood." — *PT*, 14

The Right to Choose Freely One's State in Life

Human beings have also the right to choose for themselves the kind of life which appeals to them: whether it is to found a family — in the founding of which both the man and the woman enjoy equal rights and duties — or to embrace the priesthood or the religious life.

The family, founded upon marriage freely contracted, one and indissoluble, must be regarded as the natural, primary cell of human society. The interests of the family, therefore, must be taken very specially into consideration in social and economic affairs, as well as in the spheres of faith and morals. For all of these have to do with strengthening the family and assisting it in the fulfillment of its mission.

Of course, the support and education of children is a right which belongs primarily to the parents. — *PT*, 15–17

Economic Rights

In the economic sphere, it is evident that a man has the inherent right not only to be given the opportunity to work, but also to be allowed the exercise of personal initiative in the work he does.

The conditions in which a man works form a necessary corollary to these rights. They must not be such as to weaken his physical or moral fiber or militate against the proper development of adolescents to manhood. Women must be accorded such conditions of work as are consistent with their needs and responsibilities as wives and mothers.

A further consequence of man's personal dignity is his right to engage in economic activities suited to his degree of responsibility. The worker is likewise entitled to a wage that is determined in accordance with the precepts of justice. This needs stressing. The amount a worker receives must be sufficient, in proportion to available funds, to allow him and his family a standard of living consistent with human dignity. Pope Pius XII expressed it in these terms: "Nature imposes work upon man as a duty, and man has the corresponding natural right to demand that the work he does shall provide him with the means of livelihood for himself and his children. Such is nature's categorical imperative for the preservation of man."

As a further consequence of man's nature, he has the right to the private ownership of property, including that of productive goods. This, as We have said elsewhere, is "a right which constitutes so efficacious a means of asserting one's personality and exercising responsibility in every field, and an element of solidity and security for family life, and of greater peace and prosperity in the state."

Finally, it is opportune to point out that the right to own private property entails a social obligation as well.   — PT, 18–22

The Right of Meeting and Association

Men are by nature social, and consequently they have the right to meet together and to form associations with their fellows. They have the right to confer on such associations the type of organization which they consider best calculated to achieve their objectives. They have also the right to exercise their own initiative and act on their own responsibility within these associations for the attainment of the desired results.

As We insisted in Our encyclical *Mater et Magistra,* the founding of a great many such intermediate groups or societies for the pursuit of aims which it is not within the competence of the individual to achieve efficiently, is a matter of great urgency. Such groups and societies must be considered absolutely essential for the safeguarding of man's personal freedom and dignity, while leaving intact a sense of responsibility.   —*PT,* 23–24

The Right to Emigrate and Immigrate

Again, every human being has the right to freedom of movement and of residence within the confines of his own state. When there are just reasons in favor of it, he must be permitted to emigrate to other countries and take up residence there. The fact that he is a citizen of a particular state does not deprive him of membership in the human family, nor of citizenship in that universal society, the common, worldwide fellowship of men.   —*PT,* 25

Political Rights

Finally, man's personal dignity involves his right to take an active part in public life and to make his own contribution to the common welfare of his fellow citizens. As Pope Pius XII said, "Man as such, far from being an object or, as it were, an inert element in society, is rather its subject, its basis, and its purpose; and so must he be esteemed."

As a human person he is entitled to the legal protection of his rights, and such protection must be effective, unbiased, and strictly just. To quote again Pope Pius XII: "In consequence of that juridical order willed by God, man has his own inalienable right to juridical security. To him is assigned a certain well-defined sphere of law, immune from arbitrary attack."   — *PT*, 26–27

Duties

The natural rights of which We have so far been speaking are inextricably bound up with as many duties, all applying to one and the same person. These rights and duties derive their origin, their sustenance, and their indestructibility from the natural law, which in conferring the one imposes the other.

Thus, for example, the right to live involves the duty to preserve one's life; the right to a decent standard of living, the duty to live in a becoming fashion; the right to be free to seek out the truth, the duty to devote oneself to an ever deeper and wider search for it.   — *PT*, 28–29

Reciprocity of Rights and Duties between Persons

Once this is admitted, it follows that in human society one man's natural right gives rise to a corresponding duty in other men, the duty, that is, of recognizing and respecting that right. Every basic human right draws its authoritative force from the natural law, which confers it and attaches to it its respective duty. Hence, to claim one's rights and ignore one's duties, or only half fulfill them, is like building a house with one hand and tearing it down with the other.   — *PT*, 30

Mutual Collaboration

Since men are social by nature, they must live together and consult each other's interests. That men should recognize and perform their respective rights and duties is imperative to a well-ordered society. But the result will be that each individual will make his whole-hearted contribution to the creation of a civic order in which rights and duties are ever more diligently and more effectively observed.

For example, it is useless to admit that a man has a right to the necessities of life, unless we also do all in our power to supply him with means sufficient for his livelihood.

Hence society must not only be well ordered; it must also provide men with abundant resources. This postulates not only the mutual recognition and fulfillment of rights and duties, but also the involvement and collaboration of all men in the many enterprises which our present civilization makes possible, encourages, or indeed demands. — *PT,* 31–33

An Attitude of Responsibility

Man's personal dignity requires besides that he enjoy freedom and be able to make up his own mind when he acts. In his association with his fellows, therefore, there is every reason why his recognition of rights, observance of duties, and many-sided collaboration with other men should be primarily a matter of his own personal decision. Each man should act on his own initiative, conviction, and sense of responsibility, not under the constant pressure of external coercion or enticement. There is nothing human about a society that is welded together by force. Far from encouraging, as it should, the attainment of man's progress and perfection, it is merely an obstacle to his freedom. — *PT,* 34

Reconciliation and Protection of Rights and Duties of Individuals

One of the principal duties of any government, moreover, is the suitable and adequate superintendence and coordination of men's respective rights in society. This must be done in such a way

(1) that the exercise of their rights by certain citizens does not obstruct other citizens in the exercise of theirs; (2) that the individual, standing upon his own rights, does not impede others in the performance of their duties; (3) that the rights of all be effectively safeguarded and completely restored if they have been violated.   — *PT,* 62

Duty of Promoting the Rights of Individuals

In addition, heads of state must make a positive contribution to the creation of an overall climate in which the individual can both safeguard his own rights and fulfill his duties, and can do so readily. For if there is one thing we have learned in the school of experience, it is surely this: that, in the modern world especially, political, economic, and cultural inequities among citizens become more and more widespread when public authorities fail to take appropriate action in these spheres. And the consequence is that human rights and duties are thus rendered totally ineffective.   — *PT,* 63

Characteristics of the Present Day

There is every indication at the present time that these aims and ideals are giving rise to various demands concerning the juridical organization of states. The first is this: that a clear and precisely worded charter of fundamental human rights be formulated and incorporated into the state's general constitutions.

Secondly, each state must have a public constitution, couched in juridical terms, laying down clear rules relating to the designation of public officials, their reciprocal relations, spheres of competence, and prescribed methods of operation.

The final demand is that relations between citizens and public authorities be described in terms of rights and duties. It must be clearly laid down that the principal function of public authorities is to recognize, respect, coordinate, safeguard and promote citizens' rights and duties.

We must, however, reject the view that the will of the individual or the group is the primary and only source of a citizen's rights and duties, and of the binding force of political constitutions and the government's authority.

But the aspirations We have mentioned are a clear indication of the fact that men, increasingly aware nowadays of their personal dignity, have found the incentive to enter government service and demand constitutional recognition for their own inviolable rights. Not content with this, they are demanding, too, the observance of constitutional procedures in the appointment of public authorities and are insisting that they exercise their office within this constitutional framework.   — *PT*, 75–79

ORDER IN THE UNIVERSE AND ORDER IN HUMAN BEINGS

Order in the Universe

That a marvelous order predominates in the world of living beings and in the forces of nature is the plain lesson which the progress of modern research and the discoveries of technology teach us. And it is part of the greatness of man that he can appreciate that order and devise the means for harnessing those forces for his own benefit.

But what emerges first and foremost from the progress of scientific knowledge and the inventions of technology is the infinite greatness of God himself, who created both man and the universe. Yes; out of nothing he made all things, and filled them with the fullness of his own wisdom and goodness. Hence, these are the words the holy psalmist used in praise of God: "O Lord, our Lord: how admirable is thy name in the whole earth!" (Ps.

8:1). And elsewhere he says: "How great are thy works, O Lord! Thou hast made all things in wisdom" (Ps. 103:24).

Moreover, God created man "in his own image and likeness" (Gen. 1:26), endowed him with intelligence and freedom, and made him lord of creation. All this the psalmist proclaims when he says: "Thou hast made him a little less than the angels: thou hast crowned him with glory and honor, and hast set him over the works of thy hands. Thou hast subjected all things under his feet" (Ps. 8:5–6).   — *PT,* 2–3

Order in Human Beings

And yet there is a disunity among individuals and among nations which is in striking contrast to this perfect order in the universe. One would think that the relationships that bind men together could only be governed by force.

But the world's Creator has stamped man's inmost being with an order revealed to man by his conscience; and his conscience insists on his preserving it. Men "show the work of the law written in their hearts. Their conscience bears witness to them" (Rom. 2:15). And how could it be otherwise? All created being reflects the infinite wisdom of God. It reflects it all the more clearly, the higher it stands in the scale of perfection (see Ps. 18:8–11).

But the mischief is often caused by erroneous opinions. Many people think that the laws which govern man's relations with the state are the same as those which regulate the blind, elemental forces of the universe. But it is not so; the laws which govern men are quite different. The Father of the universe has inscribed them in man's nature, and that is where we must look for them; there and nowhere else.

These laws clearly indicate how a man must behave toward his fellows in society, and how the mutual relationships between the members of a state and its officials are to be conducted. They show too what principles must govern the relations between states; and finally, what should be the relations between individuals or states on the one hand, and the worldwide community of nations on the other. Men's common interests make it imperative that at long last a worldwide community of nations be established.   — *PT,* 4–7

ORDER BETWEEN MEN

We must devote our attention first of all to that order which should prevail among men.

Any well-regulated and productive association of men in society demands the acceptance of one fundamental principle: that each individual man is truly a person. His is a nature, that is, endowed with intelligence and free will. As such he has rights and duties, which together flow as a direct consequence from his nature. These rights and duties are universal and inviolable, and therefore altogether inalienable.

When, furthermore, we consider man's personal dignity from the standpoint of divine revelation, inevitably our estimate of it is incomparably increased. Men have been ransomed by the blood of Jesus Christ. Grace has made them sons and friends of God, and heirs to eternal glory.   — *PT,* 8–10

God and the Moral Order

Now the order which prevails in human society is wholly incorporeal in nature. Its foundation is truth, and it must be brought into effect by justice. It needs to be animated and perfected by men's love for one another, and, while preserving freedom intact, it must make for an equilibrium in society which is increasingly more human in character.

But such an order — universal, absolute, and immutable in its principles — finds its source in the true, personal, and transcendent God. He is the first truth, the sovereign good, and as such the deepest source from which human society, if it is to be properly constituted, creative, and worthy of man's dignity, draws its genuine vitality. This is what St. Thomas means when he says: "Human reason is the standard which measures the degree of goodness of the human will, and as such it derives from the eternal law, which is divine reason.... Hence it is clear that the goodness of the human will depends much more on the eternal law than on human reason."   — *PT,* 37–38

An Appeal to Conscience

Hence, a regime which governs solely or mainly by means of threats and intimidation or promises of reward provides men with no effective incentive to work for the common good. And even if it did, it would certainly be offensive to the dignity of free and rational human beings. Authority is before all else a moral force. For this reason the appeal of rulers should be to the individual conscience, to the duty which every man has of voluntarily contributing to the common good. But since all men are equal in natural dignity, no man has the capacity to force internal compliance on another. Only God can do that, for he alone scrutinizes and judges the secret counsels of the heart.

Hence, representatives of the state have no power to bind men in conscience, unless their own authority is tied to God's authority, and is a participation in it.

The application of this principle likewise safeguards the dignity of citizens. Their obedience to civil authorities is never an obedience paid to them as men. It is in reality an act of homage paid to God, the provident Creator of the universe, who has decreed that men's dealings with one another be regulated in accordance with that order which he himself has established. And we men do not demean ourselves in showing due reverence to God. On the contrary, we are lifted up and ennobled in spirit, for to serve God is to reign.

Governmental authority, therefore, is a postulate of the moral order and derives from God. Consequently, laws and decrees passed in contravention of the moral order, and hence of the divine will, can have no binding force in conscience, since "it is right to obey God rather than men" (Acts 5:29).

Indeed, the passing of such laws undermines the very nature of authority and results in shameful abuse. As St. Thomas teaches, "In regard to the second proposition, we maintain that human law has the rationale of law insofar as it is in accordance with right reason, and as such it obviously derives from eternal law. A law which is at variance with reason is to that extent unjust and has no longer the rationale of law. It is rather an act of violence."

The fact that authority comes from God does not mean that men have no power to choose those who are to rule the state, or to decide upon the type of government they want, and determine the procedure and limitations of rulers in the exercise of their authority. Hence the above teaching is consonant with any genuinely democratic form of government.   *— PT,* 48–52

In Justice

Relations between states must furthermore be regulated by justice. This necessitates both the recognition of their mutual rights, and, at the same time, the fulfillment of their respective duties.

States have the right to existence, to self-development, and to the means necessary to achieve this. They have the right to play the leading part in the process of their own development, and the right to their good name and due honors. Consequently, states are likewise in duty bound to safeguard all such rights effectively, and to avoid any action that could violate them. And just as individual men may not pursue their own private interests in a way that is unfair and detrimental to others, so too it would be criminal in a state to aim at improving itself by the use of methods which involve other nations in injury and unjust oppression. There is a saying of St. Augustine which has particular relevance in this context: "Take away justice, and what are kingdoms but mighty bands of robbers."

There may be, and sometimes is, a clash of interests among states, each striving for its own development. When differences of this sort arise, they must be settled in a truly human way, not by armed force nor by deceit or trickery. There must be a mutual assessment of the arguments and feelings on both sides, a mature and objective investigation of the situation, and an equitable reconciliation of opposing views.   — *PT*, 91–93

The Treatment of Minorities

A special instance of this clash of interests is furnished by that political trend (which since the nineteenth century has become widespread throughout the world and has gained in strength) as a result of which men of similar ethnic background are anxious for political autonomy and unification into a single nation. For many reasons this cannot always be effected, and consequently minority peoples are often obliged to live within the territories of a nation of a different ethnic origin. This situation gives rise to serious problems.

It is quite clear that any attempt to check the vitality and growth of these ethnic minorities is a flagrant violation of justice, the more so if such perverse efforts are aimed at their very extinction.

Indeed, the best interests of justice are served by those public authorities who do all they can to improve the human conditions of the members of these minority groups, especially in what concerns their language, culture, ancient traditions, and their economic activity and enterprise.   — *PT*, 94–96

Justice

Justice is born of divine wisdom and consists in giving every man his due. Our first duty then is to render to God what belongs to God — to acknowledge him as Creator, Redeemer, and Source of all life. Then we must put into practice what he taught his disciples, telling them to carry this teaching of his to the ends of the world. Two thousand years have gone by since then, and this gracious message is still passed on from one man to another, though the communication is at times interrupted or halted here and there, and often stained with the blood of the confessors of the faith. But the teaching is still alive and with us and can never be abolished.

After our duty to God we must remember our obligation to give to Caesar what belongs to Caesar. This means that, when we have first of all paid our respectful homage to the Lord in the practice of our religion, we must give due consideration to our social relations.

We live on this earth; but we live by faith, and herein lies our strength. We are working for eternity, which is not of this world, but while we prepare for this final end we must learn how to live with dignity amid the trials of this present life, always subordinating all other things to what the Lord offers us in the future life. And our hope of arriving safely in eternity rests very largely on our constant respect for the rights of our fellow men. — *PD*, 137

The Fight for Justice

It is said that the primary exercise of charity is to honor justice and act accordingly, to give every man his due, not to deny the worker his just reward, to provide for our brothers' needs and also, if need arises, and at the cost of any personal sacrifice, to fight for justice. But charity to the poor, according to the Gospel commandment, must never lose its distinctive role of preceding, accompanying, inspiring, and completing the work of justice.

Even after the much desired triumph of social justice there will always remain a wide margin for charity to the poor, for our Lord said: "You always have the poor with you."

For help given to the poor the Lord reserves his special blessings: the grace of forgiveness, and the treasures of his mercy.... There is nothing more noble and more edifying than dying poor, and doing good to others even in the act of dying. — *PD*, 142

PEACE

"Have mercy on me, O God, according to thy great mercy. . . . "

This cry reaches my ears from every part of Europe and beyond. The murderous war which is being waged on the ground, on the seas, and in the air is truly a vindication of divine justice because the sacred laws governing human society have been transgressed and violated. It has been asserted, and is still being asserted, that God is bound to preserve this or that country, or grant it invulnerability and final victory, because of the righteous people who live there or because of the good that they do. We forget that although in a certain sense God has made the nations, he has left the constitution of states to the free decisions of men. To all he has made clear the rules which govern human society: they are all to be found in the Gospel. But he has not given any guarantee of special and privileged assistance, except to the race of believers, that is, to Holy Church as such. And even his assistance to his Church, although it preserves her from final defeat, does not guarantee her immunity from trials and persecutions.

The law of life, alike for the souls of men and for nations, lays down principles of justice and universal harmony and the limits to be set to the use of wealth, enjoyments, and worldly power. When this law is violated, terrible and merciless sanctions come automatically into action. No state can escape. To each its hour. War is one of the most tremendous sanctions. It is willed not by God but by men, nations, and states, through their representatives. Earthquakes, floods, famines, and pestilences are applications of the blind laws of nature, blind because nature herself has neither intelligence nor freedom. War instead is desired by men, deliberately, in defiance of the most sacred laws. That is what makes it so evil. He who instigates war and foments it is always the "Prince of this world," who has nothing to do with Christ, the "Prince of Peace" (John 12:31; 16:11).

And while the war rages, the peoples can only turn to the Miserere and beg for the Lord's mercy, that it may outweigh his justice and with a great outpouring of grace bring the powerful men of this world to their senses and persuade them to make peace....

Patriotism, which is right and may be holy, but may also degenerate into nationalism, which in my case would be most detrimental to the dignity of my episcopal ministry, must be kept above all nationalistic disputes. The world is poisoned with morbid nationalism, built up on the basis of race and blood, in contradiction to the Gospel. In this matter especially, which is of burning topical interest, "deliver me from men of blood, O God." Here fits in most aptly the invocation: "God of my salvation": Jesus our Savior died for all nations, without distinction of race or blood, and became the first brother of the new human family, built on him and his Gospel. (*Retreat of November 25–December 1, 1940*)   —*JS*, 238–39, 251

The two great evils which are poisoning the world today are secularism and nationalism. The former is characteristic of the men in power and of lay folk in general. The latter is found even among ecclesiastics. I am convinced that the Italian priests, especially the secular clergy, are less contaminated by this than others. But I must be very watchful, both as bishop and as representative of the Holy See. It is one thing to love Italy, as I most fervently do, and quite another to display this affection in public. The holy Church which I represent is the mother of nations, all nations. Everyone with whom I come into contact must admire in the pope's representative that respect for the nationality of others, expressed with graciousness and mild judgments, which inspires universal trust. Great caution then, respectful silence, and courtesy on all occasions. It will be wise for me to insist on this line of conduct being followed by all my entourage, at home and outside. We are all more or less tainted with nationalism. The apostolic delegate must be, and must be seen to be, free from this contagion. May God help me. (*Retreat of October 25–31, 1942*)   —*JS*, 260

The religious ceremony at Castel Gandolfo on Sunday, September 10, [1961,] attended by an impressive and numerous gathering of cardinals, prelates, members of the diplomatic corps, and a great throng of the faithful from all parts of the world, was wholly concerned with the general feeling of acute anxiety about the problem of peace.

The fact that we were there in our own humble person, our voice trembling with emotion, was the central, guiding, and shining point of that meeting. Our consecrated and blessed hands raised aloft the Eucharistic Sacrifice, Jesus, our Savior and Redeemer, the Savior and Redeemer of the whole world, the King of peace for all ages and all peoples.

With our heart full of emotion and of trust in God we announced on that inspired evening our intention of encouraging further gatherings, as suitable occasions present themselves, to pray about our fundamental duty of trying to preserve the peace of the world and civilization itself. It was for this intention, and to offer an initial example, that we went a few days ago to the catacombs of San Callistus, those being the nearest to our summer residence, in order to pray: surrounded by sacred memories of our predecessors, of at least fourteen popes, and bishops and martyrs famous in history, we prayed for their intercession in heaven to assure for all nations, since all belong in some way to Christ, the great treasure of peace: "That God would vouchsafe to give peace and unity to all Christian people" (the Litany of the Saints)....

For this reason, venerable brothers and beloved children, scattered throughout the world, we wish once more this year to set before you some simple and practical considerations which the devotion of the holy rosary suggests to us, for the nourishment and strengthening of vital principles intended to guide your thought and prayer. All this as an expression of perfect and tranquil Christian piety, and with the purpose of worldwide supplication for the peace of all men and of all peoples....

In the history of the most powerful states of Europe there have been some periods of great, indeed of the greatest danger, because of series of events which have stained them with tears and blood.

Those who study the developments of political events from the historical point of view know well the influence exerted by Marian devotions in preserving the nations from the calamities which threatened them, in the restoration of prosperity and social order and in the achievement of spiritual victories. (*Apostolic letter to the bishops and faithful of the whole Catholic world, September 29, 1961*) —*JS*, 357–58, 358–59, 361

To a world, which is lost, confused, and anxious under the constant threat of new frightful conflicts, the forthcoming Council must offer a possibility for all men of good will to turn their thoughts and their intentions toward peace, a peace which can and must, above all, come from spiritual and supernatural realities, from human intelligence and conscience, enlightened and guided by God the Creator and Redeemer of humanity. (*Apostolic constitution "Humanae Salutis" in which Pope John XXIII convokes the Second Vatican Council, December 25, 1961*) —*DV*, 706

The great problem confronting the world after almost two thousand years remains unchanged. Christ is ever resplendent as the center of history and of life. Men are either with him and his Church, and then they enjoy light, goodness, order, and peace. Or else they are without him, or against him, and deliberately opposed to his Church, and then they give rise to confusion, to bitterness in human relations, and to the constant danger of fratricidal wars. (*Pope John XXIII's opening speech to the Second Vatican Council, October 11, 1962*) —*DV*, 711

Christian Peace

The appearance of peace is threefold:

Peace of the Heart: Peace is before all else an interior thing, belonging to the spirit, and its fundamental condition is a loving and filial dependence on the will of God. "Thou hast made us for Thyself, O Lord, and our heart is restless till it rests in Thee" (St. Augustine's *Confessions*).

All that weakens, that breaks, that destroys this conformity and union of will is opposed to peace. First of all and before all is wrongdoing, sin. "Who hath resisted him and hath had peace?" (Job 9:4). Peace is the happy legacy of those who keep the divine law. "Much peace have they who love thy law" (Ps. 118:165).

For its part, good will is only the sincere determination to respect the eternal laws of God, to conform oneself to his commandments and to follow his paths — in a word, to abide in the truth. This is the glory which God expects to receive from man. "Peace to men of good will."

Social Peace: This is solidly based on the mutual and reciprocal respect for the personal dignity of man. The Son of God was made man, and his redeeming act concerns not only the collectivity, but also the individual man.

He "loved me and gave himself up for me." Thus spoke St. Paul to the Galatians (Gal. 2:20). And if God has loved man to such a degree, that indicates that man is of interest to him and that the human person has an absolute right to be respected.

Such is the teaching of the Church which, for the solution of these social questions, has always fixed her gaze on the human person and has taught that things and institutions — goods, the economy, the state — are primarily for man; not man for them.

The disturbances which unsettle the internal peace of nations trace their origins chiefly to this source: that man has been treated almost exclusively as a machine, a piece of merchandise, a worthless cog in some great machine or a mere productive unit.

It is only when the dignity of the person comes to be taken as the standard of value for man and his activities that the means will exist to settle civil discord and the often profound divisions between, for example, employers and the employed. Above all, it is only then that the means will exist to secure for the institution of the family those conditions of life, work, and assistance which are capable of making it better directed to its function as a cell of society and the first community instituted by God himself for the development of the human person.

No peace will have solid foundations unless hearts nourish the sentiment of brotherhood which ought to exist among all who have a common origin and are called to the same destiny. The knowledge that they belong to the same family extinguishes lust, greed, pride, and the instinct to dominate others, which are the roots of dissensions and wars. It binds all in a single bond of higher and more fruitful solidarity.

International Peace: The basis of international peace is, above all, truth. For in international relations, too, the Christian saying is valid: "The truth shall make you free" (John 8:32).

It is necessary, then, to overcome certain erroneous ideas: the myths of force, of nationalism, or of other things that have prevented the integrated life of nations. And it is necessary to impose a peaceful living together on moral principles, according to the teaching of right reason and of Christian doctrine.

Along with this, and enlightened by truth, should come justice. This removes the causes of quarrels and wars, solves the disputes, fixes the tasks, defines the duties, and gives the answer to the claims of each party.

Justice in its turn ought to be integrated and sustained by Christian charity. That is, love for one's neighbor and one's own people ought not to be concentrated on one's self in an exclusive egotism which is suspicious of another's good. But it ought to expand and reach out spontaneously toward the community of interests, to embrace all peoples and to interweave common human relations. Thus it will be possible to speak of living together, and not of mere coexistence which, precisely because it is deprived of this inspiration of mutual dependence, raises barriers behind which nestle mutual suspicion, fear, and terror.   — CM

Errors of Man in His Search for Peace

Peace is a gift of God beyond compare. Likewise, it is the object of man's highest desire. It is moreover indivisible. None of the lineaments which make up its unmistakable appearance can be ignored or excluded.

In addition, since the men of our time have not completely carried into effect the conditions of peace, the result has been that God's paths toward peace have no meeting point with those of man. Hence there is the abnormal situation of this postwar period which has created, as it were, two blocs with all their uneasy conditions. There is not a state of war, but neither is there peace, the thing which the nations ardently desire.

At all times, because true peace is indivisible in its various aspects, it will not succeed in establishing itself on the social and international planes unless it is also, and in the first place, an interior fact. This requires then before all else — it is necessary to repeat — "men of good will." These are precisely those to whom the angels of Bethlehem announced peace: "Peace among men of good will" (Luke 2:14). Indeed they alone can give reality to the conditions contained in the definition of peace given by St. Thomas: The ordered harmony of citizens and therefore order and harmony.

But how will true peace be able to put forth the two-fold blossom of order and concord if the persons who hold positions of public responsibility, before selecting the advantages and risks of their decisions, fail to recognize themselves as persons subject to the eternal moral laws?

It will be necessary again and again to remove from the path the obstacles placed by the malice of man. And the presence of these obstacles is noted in the propaganda of immorality, in social injustice, in forced unemployment, in poverty contrasted with the luxury of those who can indulge in dissipation, in the dreadful lack of proportion between the technical and moral progress of nations, and in the unchecked armaments race, where there has yet to be a glimpse of a serious possibility of solving the problem of disarmament.   —CM

The Work of the Church

. . . It is a function and office proper to the Church that it should devote itself to peace. And the Church is aware of having omitted nothing that was within its capacities to obtain peace for nations and individuals. The Church looks with favor on every initiative which can help to spare humanity new conflicts, new massacres, and incalculable new destruction.

Unfortunately, the causes which have disturbed, and now disturb, international order have not yet been removed. It is therefore necessary to dry up the sources of evil. Otherwise the dangers to peace will remain a constant threat.

The causes of international sickness were clearly proclaimed by Our predecessor, Pius XII of immortal memory, especially in his Christmas messages of 1942 and 1943. It is well to repeat them.

These causes are: the violation of the rights and dignity of the human person and the overruling of the rights of the family and of labor; the overthrow of the juridical order and of the healthy idea of the state in keeping with the Christian spirit; impairment of the liberty, integrity, and security of other nations to whatever extent; the systematic oppression of the cultural and language characteristics of national minorities; the egotistical calculations of all who strive to seize control of the economic sources of the materials of common use to the detriment of other peoples; and in particular, the persecution of religion and of the Church. . . .

At Bethlehem all men must find their place. In the first rank should be Catholics. Today especially the Church wishes to see them pledged to an effort to make his message of peace a part of themselves. And the message is an invitation to check the direction of every act by the dictates of divine law, which demands the unflinching adherence of all, even to the point of sacrifice. Along with such a deepened understanding must go action. It is utterly intolerable for Catholics to restrict themselves to the position of mere observers. They should feel clothed, as it were, with a mandate from on high.

The pope's task is to prepare for God a perfect people (Luke 1:17), which is exactly like the task of [John] the Baptist, who is his patron and from whom he takes his name. And it is not possible to imagine a higher and more precious perfection than that of Christian peace, which is the peace of hearts, peace in the social order, in life, in prosperity, in mutual respect, and in the brotherhood of all nations.   — CM

Peace on Earth — which man throughout the ages has so longed for and sought after — can never be established, never guaranteed, except by the diligent observance of the divinely established order.   — PT, 1

Causes of the Arms Race

On the other hand, We are deeply distressed to see the enormous stocks of armaments that have been, and continue to be, manufactured in the economically more developed countries. This policy is involving a vast outlay of intellectual and material resources, with the result that the people of these countries are saddled with a great burden, while other countries lack the help they need for their economic and social development.

There is a common belief that under modern conditions peace cannot be assured except on the basis of an equal balance of armaments and that this factor is the probable cause of this stockpiling of armaments. Thus, if one country increases its military strength, others are immediately roused by a competitive spirit to augment their own supply of armaments. And if one country is equipped with atomic weapons, others consider themselves justified in producing such weapons themselves, equal in destructive force.

Consequently people are living in the grip of constant fear. They are afraid that at any moment the impending storm may break upon them with horrific violence. And they have good reasons for their fear, for there is certainly no lack of such weapons. While it is difficult to believe that anyone would dare to assume responsibility for initiating the appalling slaughter and destruction that war would bring in its wake, there is no denying that the conflagration could be started by some chance and unforeseen circumstance. Moreover, even though the monstrous power of modern weapons does indeed act as a deterrent, there is reason to fear that the very testing of nuclear devices for war purposes can, if continued, lead to serious danger for various forms of life on earth. — *PT,* 109–11

Need for Disarmament

Hence justice, right reason, and the recognition of man's dignity cry out insistently for a cessation to the arms race. The stockpiles of armaments which have been built up in various countries must be reduced all round and simultaneously by the parties concerned. Nuclear weapons must be banned. A general agreement must be reached on a suitable disarmament program, with an effective system of mutual control. In the words of Pope Pius XII: "The calamity of a world war, with the economic and social ruin and the moral excesses and dissolution that accompany it, must not on any account be permitted to engulf the human race for a third time."

Everyone, however, must realize that, unless this process of disarmament be thoroughgoing and complete, and reach men's very souls, it is impossible to stop the arms race, or to reduce armaments, or — and this is the main thing — ultimately to abolish them entirely. Everyone must sincerely cooperate in the effort to banish fear and the anxious expectation of war from men's minds. But this requires that the fundamental principles upon which peace is based in today's world be replaced by an altogether different one, namely, the realization that true and lasting peace among nations cannot consist in the possession of an equal supply of armaments but only in mutual trust. And We are confident that this can be achieved, for it is a thing which not only is dictated by common sense, but is in itself most desirable and most fruitful of good.   — *PT,* 112–13

Signs of the Times

Men nowadays are becoming more and more convinced that any disputes which may arise between nations must be resolved by negotiation and agreement, and not by recourse to arms.

We acknowledge that this conviction owes its origin chiefly to the terrifying destructive force of modern weapons. It arises from fear of the ghastly and catastrophic consequences of their use. Thus, in this age which boasts of its atomic power, it no longer makes sense to maintain that war is a fit instrument with which to repair the violation of justice.

And yet, unhappily, we often find the law of fear reigning supreme among nations and causing them to spend enormous sums on armaments. Their object is not aggression, so they say — and there is no reason for disbelieving them — but to deter others from aggression.

Nevertheless, We are hopeful that, by establishing contact with one another and by a policy of negotiation, nations will come to a better recognition of the natural ties that bind them together as men. We are hopeful, too, that they will come to a fairer realization of one of the cardinal duties deriving from our common nature: namely, that love, not fear, must dominate the relationships between individuals and between nations. It is principally characteristic of love that it draws men together in all sorts of ways, sincerely united in the bonds of mind and matter; and this is a union from which countless blessings can flow. — *PT,* 126–29

Interior Peace

The world will never be the dwelling place of peace, till peace has found a home in the heart of each and every man, till every man preserves in himself the order ordained by God to be preserved. That is why St. Augustine asks the question: "Does your mind desire the strength to gain the mastery over your passions? Let it submit to a greater power, and it will conquer all beneath it. And peace will be in you — true, sure, most ordered peace. What is that order? God as ruler of the mind; the mind as ruler of the body. Nothing could be more orderly."   — *PT,* 165

The Prince of Peace

Our concern here has been with problems which are causing men extreme anxiety at the present time, problems which are intimately bound up with the progress of human society. Unquestionably, the teaching We have given has been inspired by a longing which We feel most keenly, and which We know is shared by all men of good will: that peace may be assured on earth.

We who, in spite of Our inadequacy, are nevertheless the vicar of him whom the prophet announced as the Prince of Peace [see Isa. 9:6], conceive of it as Our duty to devote all Our thoughts and care and energy to further this common good of all mankind. Yet peace is but an empty word, if it does not rest upon that order which Our hope prevailed upon Us to set forth in outline in this encyclical. It is an order that is founded on truth, built up on justice, nurtured and animated by charity, and brought into effect under the auspices of freedom.

So magnificent, so exalted is this aim that human resources alone, even though inspired by the most praiseworthy good will, cannot hope to achieve it. God himself must come to man's aid with his heavenly assistance, if human society is to bear the closest possible resemblance to the kingdom of God.

The very order of things, therefore, demands that during this sacred season we pray earnestly to him who by his bitter passion and death washed away men's sins, which are the fountainhead of discord, misery and inequality; to him who shed his blood to reconcile the human race to the heavenly Father, and bestowed the gifts of peace. "For he is our peace, who hath made both one.... And coming, he preached peace to you that were afar off; and peace to them that were nigh" (Eph. 2:14–17).

The sacred liturgy of these days reechoes the same message: "Our Lord Jesus Christ, after his resurrection stood in the midst of his disciples and said: Peace be upon you, alleluia. The disciples rejoiced when they saw the Lord." It is Christ, therefore, who brought us peace; Christ who bequeathed it to us: "Peace I leave with you: my peace I give unto you: not as the world giveth, do I give unto you" (John 14:27).

Let us, then, pray with all fervor for this peace which our divine Redeemer came to bring us. May he banish from the souls of men whatever might endanger peace. May he transform all men into witnesses of truth, justice, and brotherly love. May he illumine with his light the minds of rulers, so that, besides caring for the proper material welfare of their peoples, they may also guarantee them the fairest gift of peace.

Finally, may Christ inflame the desires of all men to break through the barriers which divide them, to strengthen the bonds of mutual love, to learn to understand one another, and to pardon those who have done them wrong. Through his power and inspiration may all peoples welcome each other to their hearts as brothers, and may the peace they long for ever flower and ever reign among them.   — *PT,* 166–71

5

Prayers and Devotions

*The declaration "Apart from me you can do nothing" (John 15:5)
that Jesus addressed to his followers applies to Pope John XXIII
as it applies to every Christian. Pope John was a man of prayer.
He wrote: "I must, I will, become increasingly a man of intense
prayer.... My day must be one long prayer: prayer is the breath
of my life" (JS, 210, 283). He lived a life of prayer. He prayed
the traditional prayers and did the regular spiritual exercises and
devotions. He also prayed personal prayers that he himself wrote
and shared with others. His prayers were an edifying example of
intimacy with God and abandonment to divine providence. Also,
he had a special devotion for the Virgin Mary, the Mother of God
and our Mother. He knew that by himself he "can do nothing,"
but "[he] can do all things through him who strengthens [him]"
(Phil. 4:13).*

A Prayer That the Will of God May Be Fulfilled

O most merciful Jesus, grant to me your grace, "that it may be
with me, and labor with me" [Wisd. 9:10] and persevere with
me even to the end. Grant that I may always desire and will that
which is to you most acceptable and most dear.

Let your will be mine, and let my will ever respond to yours,
in perfect accordance. Let me desire what you desire and hate

what you hate, and let me desire and hate nothing but what you desire and hate. Let me die to all that is of this world and for your sake rejoice to be despised and ignored in this generation. Grant me, above all other desires, the desire to rest in you, that my heart may find its peace in you. You are the true peace of the heart, you are its only resting place; apart from you all things are harsh and restless. In this peace, in this very peace which is yourself, the one supreme, eternal Good, I will sleep and rest. Amen (Thomas à Kempis, *The Imitation of Christ*). (*1895*)

—*JS*, 10–11

Prayer to Jesus Christ

O Lord Jesus Christ, who have deigned to call me, Angelo Giuseppe, your poor unworthy servant, to the life of a priest, not through any merits of my own but out of your charity alone, grant me I beseech you, through the intercession of my most holy and beloved Mother, Mary Immaculate, and of all my holy patron saints, to whose care I commend myself, that I, like your beloved John, burning with the fire of your charity and adorned with all virtues, especially humility, may be able to consecrate my soul and body and all my doings to the greater glory of your name, and that of your spouse the Catholic Church, and to inflame the hearts of all men with your love so that they may choose you alone and serve you alone. May there be restored on earth your kingdom of which you are the eternal King, full of the blessings of charity and peace, you who with God the Father in the unity of the Holy Spirit live and reign, world without end. Amen. (*1895*)

—*JS*, 11

Knight of Christ

Hail, Christ the King! You summon me to fight your battles and, without a moment's delay, with all the enthusiasm of my twenty years and the grace you have given me, I boldly enlist in the ranks of your volunteers. I dedicate myself to your service, for life or death. You offer me your Cross for a standard and a weapon. I place my right hand on this invincible weapon and give you my solemn word, swearing with all the fervor of my youthful heart absolute fidelity until death. So I, whom you created your servant, have become your soldier. I put on your uniform, I gird on your sword, I am proud to call myself a knight of Christ. Give me a soldier's heart, a knight's velour, O Jesus, and I will always be by your side in the rough moments of life, in sacrifices, in ordeals, in battles — and still with you in the hour of victory. And since the signal for the fight has not yet sounded for me, while I remain in my tent, waiting for my hour to strike, you must teach me by your shining example how to try out my velour against my own interior enemies, so as to get rid of these first. They are so many, O Jesus, and they are without mercy! There is one especially who is up to every trick; he is proud and cunning, he clings to me, he pretends to want to make peace and then he makes fun of me, he offers terms, he even follows me into my good deeds.

Lord Jesus, you know who that is: my self-love, the spirit of pride, presumption, and vanity. Help me to get rid of him once and for all or, if that is not possible, at least to hold him in subjection so that, unhampered in my movements, I may run to the breach, stand among the warriors who defend your holy cause and sing with you the hymn of salvation. (*From notes made during the Spiritual Exercises of December 10–20, 1902*) —*JS,* 89

On Christmas Night

Night has fallen; the clear bright stars are sparkling in the cold air; noisy strident voices rise to my ear from the city, voices of the revelers of this world who celebrate with their merrymaking the poverty of their Savior. Around me in their rooms my companions are asleep, and I am still wakeful, thinking of the mystery of Bethlehem.

Come, come Jesus, I await you.

Mary and Joseph, knowing the hour is near, are turned away by the townsfolk and go out into the fields to look for a shelter. I am a poor shepherd, I have only a wretched stable, a small manger, some wisps of straw. I offer all these to you; be pleased to come into my poor hovel. Make haste, O Jesus, I offer you my heart; my soul is poor and bare of virtues, the straws of so many imperfections will prick you and make you weep — but O my Lord what can you expect? This little is all I have. I am touched by your poverty, I am moved to tears, but I have nothing better to offer you. Jesus, honor my soul with your presence, adorn it with your graces. Burn this straw and change it into a soft couch for your most holy body.

Jesus, I am here waiting for your coming. Wicked men have driven you out and the wind is like ice. Come into my heart. I am a poor man but I will warm you as well as I can. At least be pleased that I wish to welcome you warmly, to love you dearly and sacrifice myself for you.

But in your own way you are rich and you see my needs. You are a flame of charity and you will purge my heart of all that is not your own most holy Heart. You are uncreated holiness and you will fill me with those graces which give new life to my soul. O Jesus, come, I have so much to tell you, so many sorrows to confide, so many desires, so many promises, so many hopes.

I want to adore you, to kiss you on the brow, O tiny Jesus, to give myself to you once more, forever. Come, my Jesus, delay no longer; come, be my guest.

Alas! It is already late, I am overcome with sleep and my pen slips from my fingers. Let me sleep a little, O Jesus, while your Mother and St. Joseph are preparing the room.

I will lie down to rest here, in the fresh night air. As soon as you come the splendor of your light will dazzle my eyes. Your angels will awaken me with sweet hymns of glory and peace and I shall run forward with joy to welcome you and to offer you my own poor gifts, my home, all the little I have. I will worship you and show you all my love, with the other shepherds who have joined

me and with the angels of heaven, singing hymns of glory to your Sacred Heart. Come, I am longing for you. (*December 24, 1902*)
— *JS, 99–100*

A Man of Intense Prayer

I must, I will, become increasingly a man of intense prayer. This last year has brought some improvement in this direction. I shall continue with perseverance and fervor, giving even greater attention and importance to my religious duties: Holy Mass, the Breviary, Bible reading, meditation, examination of conscience, the rosary, the visit to the Blessed Sacrament. Jesus in the Blessed Sacrament is reserved in my house, and he is my joy. May he ever find in my home and in my life something to gladden his divine heart. (*Retreat of November 9–13, 1927*) — *JS, 210*

To the Child Jesus

O heavenly Child, our almighty Lord, we believe that you grant the requests of those who turn to you with pure hearts and that you also hear the prayers of those who are silent; we thank you for having called us today to share in the holy mysteries offered to our souls, to strengthen us ever more in the faith, to preserve our piety, and to obtain for us forgiveness of our sins. Your name has been invoked over us.

Keep us closely united among ourselves and with those who are dedicated to your service. Confirm us in your truth, through the grace of the Holy Spirit; reveal to us the truths of which we are still ignorant, supply what we lack, and strengthen our faith in what we know. Preserve priests in purity for the service of your altar, and protect kings and governments in peace and magistrates in justice; give us tranquil skies and the fruits of the earth in abundance, and keep the whole world in your almighty care. Calm aggressive minds, convert the erring, make your people holy, preserve the purity of virgins, guard the faith-fulness of married men and women, fortify the chaste; enlighten those who have only just begun to follow your teaching, and confirm them, make them worthy of loftier attainment, and may we at the last all be eternally reunited in your kingdom, O Jesus, together with you, with the Father and the Holy Spirit, to whom be glory, honor and blessing forever and ever. Amen. (*Prayer taken from his Christmas homily, Sofia, 1929*)   —*JS*, 377

The Breath of Life

During this retreat I have been reading St. Gregory and St. Ber-nard, both of them concerned with the *interior life* of the pastor, which must not be affected by external material cares. My day must be one long prayer: prayer is the breath of my life. I propose to recite all fifteen decades of the rosary every day, if possible in the chapel before the Blessed Sacrament, with the intention of recommending to Our Lord and to Our Lady the more urgent needs of my children in Venice and in the diocese: the clergy, young seminarians, consecrated virgins, public authorities, and poor sinners. (*Retreat of May 15–21, 1953*)   —*JS*, 283

O Mary, Queen of the Lebanon

Now, O Mary, Queen of the Lebanon and recently proclaimed Queen of the World, hear my prayer. The archangel who was the first to greet you called you "full of grace." A great Doctor of the Church, St. Bernard, commented: "You are full of grace and your grace overflows to us: you have more than enough grace for yourself, enough to spare for us."

O Mary, pour out the superabundance of your grace over this beloved nation of yours. For the fist time in its long history it enjoys full liberty and political and social independence. May its decrees be ever inspired by principles of respect and fidelity for its glorious ancestral traditions; may its social life be characterized by those mystical gifts of unity and peace which are the most fervent intention of the holy Sacrifice of the Mass which I am now celebrating under your loving gaze of O Mother, O Queen of the Lebanon, in close sacrificial union with blessed Jesus, your Son and our Brother.

One more prayer, O Mary. In answer to the prayer of Jesus that all his brothers should be united among themselves and with him, as he is united with the Father (see John 17:23), the promise of one fold under the pastoral staff of one shepherd (John 10:16) will surely be fulfilled; let the attainment of this unity for which all believers in Christ are longing begin here, in the land of the Lebanon, through your intercession, O Mary!

The restoration of the catholicity of faith in all its breadth and perfection will be the most important event of modern times. May it be ascribed to your name, O Queen of the Lebanon, as our Holy Father says in the words which I shall transmit to these your faithful people in his name. The pope will say to the Lebanese: "Your fervor, renewed in these devotions to Mary, must be the salt that does not lose its savor, the light set on a candlestick so that its flame may be a light to all that are in the house. May the warmth of your charity be shown above all in welcoming your separated brethren, whose deep devotion to Mary is well known to us, and to whom in our encyclical *Fulgens Corona* we have sent a fatherly invitation to join with us in appealing to Mary, and begging most earnestly for this unity."

My dear Lebanese brothers, nothing is beyond the reach of prayer. The Archangel Gabriel is still here with us. The last word of his message is precisely this: "With God nothing will be impossible" (Luke 1:37).

So, courage and faith!

On the summit of the holy mountain the ancient cedars are still growing, ever growing, and their branches are still wide and robust enough to gather in a mystical embrace all who worship Christ "in spirit and in truth." This will be the future glory of Lebanon, the glory of Mary, her Mother and Queen, Amen.

(From the concluding homily of the Marian celebrations, Beirut,
October 24, 1954)   —*JS*, 381–82

Mary, Fountain of Mercy and Mother of Joy

We crown you together with your divine Son, O Madonna di
Siponto, we crown you as our Queen, and may the golden crown
that encircles your brow glow as the sign of the highest holiness to which a human creature may rise, as an "ornament of
honor" that surpasses all other dignity and merit in the Holy
Church, both militant and triumphant, and finally as a symbol of your most powerful intercession with your Son for our
needs. These are the individual needs of every one of us, of our
families, and the whole of this noble archdiocese of Manfredonia, most fortunate in having been for centuries past under
your heavenly protection, and which the presence of St. Michael,
unconquered prince of the heavenly hosts, at your command de-
fends in many and various ways against the forces of disorder and
evil, a sure safeguard against all the temptations and misfortunes
of life.

O Madonna di Siponto, come, let us crown you Queen. The
crown is of purest gold, like the hearts of your children who
offer it to you, like the heart of their pastor who procured it for
you ... "and a crown of gold upon her head, a sign of holiness,
an ornament of honor, and a work of power."

O Queen of Siponto, I beg two special graces of you: peace
of mind and the spirit of peace in our families, in our parishes,
and all this diocese which loves and honors you; peace in Italy,
our own blessed land, in all her endeavors to achieve the loftiest
ideals of human and social life in the light of the Gospel and
in faithfulness to the teaching of the apostles, today, yesterday,
and always the only shining beacon of truth, justice, and true
Christian brotherhood.

Ah my brothers! I speak of true Christian brotherhood and,
after peace, this is the second grace for which I intend to pray,

and for which I ask you all to pray to Jesus during this solemn evening ceremony, under the auspices and with the help of the prayers of the newly crowned Queen of Siponto.

This holy image comes to us almost certainly from the eastern shores of our sea. Those other numerous and similar images of Our Lady which are so greatly revered in our peninsula came to Italy from the east, during the first half of the thirteenth century. First of all our own sweet Madonna Nicopeja in St. Mark's in Venice. Here, in these parts, we have St. Mary of Constantinople in the cathedral of Bari, the Madonna of the Fountain in Trani, the Virgin of the Martyrs in Molfetta, the Madonna della Guardia in Bologna, Santa Maria Valleverde in Bovino, the Madonna of Grottaferrata, and others, all from the East and Byzantine in character and style.

O Mary, why should not your Eastern children be reunited with us, in the house of our common Father who awaits them, and so restore the "one fold and one shepherd," for which Jesus asked in his last prayer, when he was about to offer himself in sacrifice for our redemption and the peace of the whole world?

We pray that the vast regions where faith in Christ, formulated in the same apostolic Creed, still groans and suffers may find a way of peaceful return to that source of true unity of all peoples in the embrace of our common mother, in Jesus her blessed firstborn Son, and in the embrace of the other Mother we all share in common, the holy Catholic Church, to which it is our joy to belong, and which awaits the return of all.

O newly crowned Madonna di Siponto, may this your image and all the others which represent you in Italy, in the Near East and in the vast lands of Russia, inspire our prayers for this return to unity, which will be the joy and exultation of continents and seas, of earth and heaven, in Christ Jesus your Son and our Brother, to whom in our emotion we dedicate the prayers of our lips and the throbbing of our grateful joyful hearts, in the glorification of his blessed Mother and ours. (*This prayer is taken from the homily*

preached by the patriarch of Venice for the Pontifical Mass at
Manfredonia, August 28, 1955, on the occasion of the crowning
of the Madonna di Siponto.) 　　　　　　　　　　　—*JS, 383–84*

Prayer in Honor of the Eucharistic King

O Jesus, King of all peoples and all ages, accept the acts of adoration and praise which we, your brothers by adoption, humbly offer you.

You are the "living Bread which comes down from heaven and gives life to the world" (John 6:33), Supreme Priest and Victim. On the Cross you offered yourself to the Eternal Father as a bloody sacrifice of expiation, for the redemption of the human race, and now you offer yourself daily upon our altars by the hands of your ministers, in order to establish in every heart your "reign of truth and life, of holiness and grace, of justice, love and peace" (Preface of the Mass of Christ the King).

O King of glory, may your kingdom come! Reign from your "throne of grace" (Heb. 4:14), in the hearts of children, so that they may guard untainted the white lily of baptismal innocence. Reign in the hearts of the young, that they may grow up healthy and pure, obedient to the commands of those who represent you in their families and schools and in the Church. Reign in our homes, so that parents and children may live in peace in obedience to your holy law. Reign in our land, so that all citizens, in the harmonious order of the various social groups, may feel themselves children of the same heavenly Father, called to cooperate for the common good of this world, happy to belong to the one Mystical Body, of which your Sacrament is at once the symbol and the everlasting source.

Finally, reign, O King of kings and "Lord of lords" (Deut. 10:17) over all the nations of the earth, and enlighten all their rulers in order that, inspired by your example, they may make "plans for welfare and not for evil" (Jer. 29:11).

O Jesus, present in the Sacrament of the Altar, teach all the nations to serve you with willing hearts, knowing that "to serve God is to reign." May your Sacrament, O Jesus, be light to the mind, strength to the will, joy to the heart. May it be the support of the weak, the comfort of the suffering, the wayfaring bread of salvation for the dying, and for all the "pledge of future glory." Amen.   —*PD, 92–93*

Prayer for the Second Ecumenical Vatican Council

O divine Spirit, sent by the Father in the Name of Jesus, give your aid and infallible guidance to your Church and pour out on the Ecumenical Council the fullness of your gifts.

O gentle Teacher and Consoler, enlighten the hearts of our prelates who, eagerly responding to the call of the Supreme Roman Pontiff, will gather here in solemn conclave.

May this Council produce abundant fruits: may the light and power of the Gospel be more widely diffused in human society; may new vigor be imparted to the Catholic religion and its missionary function; may we all acquire a more profound knowledge of the Church's doctrine and a wholesome increase of Christian morality.

O gentle Guest of our souls, confirm our minds in truth and dispose our hearts to obedience, that the deliberations of the Council may find in us generous consent and prompt obedience.

We pray to you again for the lambs who are no longer part of the one fold of Jesus Christ, that they too, who still glory in the name of Christians, may at last be reunited under one Shepherd.

Renew in our own days your miracles as of a second Pentecost; and grant that Holy Church, reunited in one prayer, more fervent than before, around Mary the Mother of Jesus, and under the leadership of Peter, may extend the kingdom of the divine Savior, a kingdom of truth, justice, love, and peace. Amen. (*September 23, 1959*)   —*JS, 391*

A Prayer for Missionaries

O Lord, remember your missionaries, priests, nuns, and lay people, who give up all they have to testify to your Gospel and your love. Be for every one of them a powerful protector, a stronghold, a shelter in all danger, a refuge in the noonday heat, their support lest they falter, their succor when they fall! Strengthen them in moments of difficulty, fortify them, console them, crown their labor with the victories of the spirit. They do not seek success in this world, or its fleeting joys, but only your triumph and the salvation of souls.

May the sacred crucifix which accompanies them throughout their lives speak to them of heroism, of self-denial, of love, and of peace. May it be their comfort and guide, their light and strength, in order that through their endeavors your blessed Name may be made known throughout the world, and that surrounded by the ever growing numbers of your children, they may raise to you the hymn of thankfulness, redemption, and glory. Amen.

— PD, 268–69

To Mary, Queen of the World

We turn to you, O blessed Virgin Mary, Mother of Jesus and our Mother too. How could we, with trembling hearts, concern ourselves with the greatest problem of all, that of life or death, now overshadowing all mankind, without trusting ourselves to your intercession to preserve us from all dangers?

This is your hour, O Mary, Our blessed Jesus entrusted us to you in the final hour of his bloody sacrifice. We are sure that you will intervene.

On September 8, Holy Church celebrated the feast of your most blessed birth, hailing it as the beginning of the salvation of the world, and a heavenly omen for lasting peace.

And now indeed we beseech you for this, O most sweet Mother and Queen of the world. The world does not need victorious wars or defeated peoples but renewed and strengthened health of mind, and peace which brings prosperity and tranquility; this is what it needs and what it is crying out for: the beginning of salvation and lasting peace. Amen. Amen. (*From the broadcast prayer for peace among the nations, Sunday, December 10, 1961*) — *JS*, 395

Prayer to the Holy Ghost

O Holy Ghost, Paraclete, perfect in us the work begun by Jesus: enable us to continue to pray fervently in the name of the whole world: hasten in every one of us the growth of a profound interior life; give vigor to our apostolate so that it may reach all men and all peoples, all redeemed by the Blood of Christ and all belonging to him. Mortify in us our natural pride, and raise us to the realms of holy humility, of the real fear of God, of generous courage. Let no earthly bond prevent us from honoring our vocation, no cowardly consideration disturb the claims of justice, no meanness confine the immensity of charity within the narrow bounds of petty selfishness. Let everything in us be on a grand scale: the search for truth and the devotion to it, and readiness for self-sacrifice, even to the cross and death; and may everything finally be according to the last prayer of the Son to his heavenly Father, and according to your Spirit, O Holy Spirit of love, which the Father and the Son desired to be poured out over the Church and its institutions, over the souls of men and over nations. Amen. Amen. Alleluia, Alleluia! (*From the homily for Pentecost, Sunday, June 10, 1962*) — *JS*, 397

To Jesus in the Eucharistic Mystery

O Jesus, you see how from every altar and every Christian heart, prayer ascends this day with more warmth and more emotion!

O Jesus, look upon us from your Sacrament like a good Shepherd, by which name the Angelic Doctor invokes you, and with him Holy Church. O Jesus, good Shepherd, this is your flock, the flock that you have gathered from the ends of the earth, the flock that listens to your word of life, and intends to guard it, practice it, and preach it. This is the flock that follows you meekly, O Jesus, and wishes so ardently to see, in the Ecumenical Council, the reflection of your loving face in the features of your Church, the mother of all, the mother who opens her arms and heart to all, and here awaits, trembling and trustful, the arrival of all her bishops.

O Jesus, divine Food of the soul, this immense concourse turns to you. It wishes to give to its human and Christian vocation a new, vigorous power of interior virtue, and to be ready for sacrifice, of which you were such a wonderful pattern in word and in example.

You are our elder Brother; you have trodden our path before us, O Christ Jesus, the path of every one of us; you have forgiven all our sins; you inspire us each and all to give a nobler, more convinced and more active witness of Christian life.

O Jesus, our true Bread, and the only substantial Food for our souls, gather all the peoples around your table. Your altar is divine reality on earth, the pledge of heavenly favors, the assurance of a just understanding among peoples and of peaceful rivalry in the true progress of civilization.

Nourished by you and with you, O Jesus, men will be strong in faith, joyful in hope, and active in the many and varied expressions of charity.

Our wills will know how to overcome the snares of evil, the temptations of selfishness, the listlessness of sloth. And the eyes of men who love and fear the Lord will behold the vision of the land of the living, of which the wayfaring Church militant is the image, enabling the whole earth to hear the first sweet and mysterious voices of the City of God.

O Jesus, feed us and guard us, and grant that we may see the good things in the land of the living! Amen. Alleluia. (*Prayer recited after the procession of the Blessed Sacrament in St. Peter's Square, Corpus Christi, June 21, 1962*)   —*JS*, 398–99

Prayer for the Beginning of Lent

O Lord Jesus, you who at the beginning of your public life withdrew into the desert, we beg you to teach all men that recollection of mind which is the beginning of conversion and salvation.

Leaving your home at Nazareth and your sweet Mother, you wished to experience solitude, weariness, and hunger. To the tempter who proposed to you the trial of miracles, you replied with the strength of eternal wisdom, in itself a miracle of heavenly grace.

It is Lent.

O Lord, do not let us turn to "broken cisterns," which can hold no water (Jer. 2:13), not imitate the unfaithful servant or the foolish virgins; do not let us be so blinded by the enjoyment of the good things of earth that our hearts become insensible to the cry of the poor, of the sick, of orphan children, and of those innumerable brothers of ours who still lack the necessary minimum to eat, to clothe their nakedness, and to gather their family together under one roof.

You also, O Jesus, were immersed in the river of Jordan, under the eyes of the crowd, although very few then were able to recognize you; and this mystery of tardy faith, or of indifference, prolonged through the centuries, is a source of grief for those who love you and have received the mission of making you known in the world.

O grant to the successors of your apostles and disciples and to all who call themselves after your Name and your Cross, to press on with the work of spreading the Gospel and bear witness to it in prayer, suffering, and loving obedience to your will!

And since you, an innocent lamb, came before John in the attitude of a sinner, so draw us also to the waters of the Jordan. To the Jordan will we go to confess our sins and cleanse our souls. And as the skies opened to announce the voice of your Father, expressing his pleasure in you, so, having successfully overcome our trial and lived austerely through the forty days of our Lent, may we, O Jesus, when the day of your Resurrection dawns, hear once more in our innermost hearts the same heavenly Father's voice, recognizing us as his children.

O holy Lent of this mystic year of the Ecumenical Council!

May this prayer rise, on this evening of serene religious recollection, from every house where people work, love, and suffer. May the angels of heaven gather the prayers of all the souls of little children, of generous-hearted young men and women, of hard-working and self-sacrificing parents, and of all who suffer in body and mind, and present their prayers to God. From him will flow down in abundance the gifts of his heavenly joys, of which our Apostolic Benediction is a pledge and a reflection. (*From the broadcast of February 28, 1963*)   —*JS*, 402–3

6

Selected Sayings

Pope John XXIII was pope for four years, cardinal and patriarch for five years, bishop and priest for forty-nine years, and Christian for eighty-one years — all his life. His receptive and astute mind, his intuitive and kind heart, and his many years spent in different countries and cultures that allowed him to learn from practical experience as well as from books helped him to reach the wisdom and maturity known in a true spiritual master. The following short sayings of his radiate the authenticity, simplicity, humility, trust, joy, and determination found in a true disciple of Christ. They are powerful sparks of wisdom that draw us onto the path of transformation, offering us guidance in our endeavors toward the fulfillment of our destiny.

1. The whole world is my family. (*JS*, 299)

2. Everyone calls me "Holy Father," and holy I must and will be. (*JS*, 303)

3. My real greatness lies in doing the will of God, entirely and perfectly. (*JS*, 112)

4. My day must be one long prayer: prayer is the breath of my life. (*JS*, 283)

5. I must be holy at all costs. (*JS*, 94)

6. Everyone must be treated with respect, prudence, and evangelical simplicity. (*JS*, 309)

7. My obligation to aim at sanctification at all costs must be ever present in my mind. (*JS*, 111)

8. My only wish is that my life should end in a holy manner. (*JS*, 280)

9. I want to be a holy pastor. (*JS*, 283)

10. "Know thyself": this keeps me humble and without pretensions. (*JS*, 275)

11. "Having nothing" yet "possessing all things" [2 Cor. 6:10] comes true every day under my eyes. (*JS*, 194)

12. I live by the mercy of Jesus, to whom I owe everything and from whom I expect everything. (*JS*, 307)

13. The more I speak about myself the more virtue I lose; vanity squirts out from every word, even from those which seem most innocent. (*JS*, 100)

14. I really must make sure that I never tell others to do what I do not try to practice myself. (*JS*, 24)

15. Above all, I wish to continue always to render good for evil, and in all things to endeavor to prefer the Gospel truth to the wiles of human politics. (*JS*, 228)

16. All the evils which poison men and nations and trouble so many hearts have a single cause and a single source: ignorance of the truth — and at times even more than ignorance, a contempt for truth and a reckless rejection of it. (*APC*, 6)

17. Our spirit will rest in peace and joy only when we have reached that truth which is taught in the Gospels and which should be reduced to action in our lives. (*APC*, 19)

18. Mutual ties between states must be governed by truth. (*PT*, 86)

19. Laws and decrees passed in contravention of the moral order, and hence of the divine will, can have no binding force in conscience, since "it is right to obey God rather than men" (Acts 5:29). (*PT*, 51)

20. Mutual trust among rulers of states cannot begin nor increase except by recognition of, and respect for, the moral order. (*MM*, 207)

21. The most fundamental modern error is that of imagining that man's natural sense of religion is nothing more than the outcome of feeling or fantasy, to be eradicated from his soul as an anachronism and obstacle to human progress. And yet this very need of religion reveals a man for what he is: a being created by God and tending always toward God. (*MM*, 214)

22. Let men make all the technical and economic progress they can; there will be no peace or justice in the world until they return to a sense of their dignity as creatures and sons of God, who is the first and final cause of all created being. (*MM*, 215)

23. Separated from God a man is but a monster, in himself and toward others; for the right ordering of human society presupposes the right ordering of man's conscience with God, who is himself the source of all justice, truth, and love. (*MM*, 215)

24. The most perniciously typical aspect of the modern era consists in the absurd attempt to reconstruct a solid and fruitful temporal order divorced from God, who is, in fact, the only foundation on which it can endure. (*MM*, 217)

25. At all times, because true peace is indivisible in its various aspects, it will not succeed in establishing itself on the social and international planes unless it is also, and in the first place, an interior fact. (CM)

26. True peace cannot come save from God. It has only one name: the peace of Christ. (CM)

27. The basis of international peace is, above all, truth. For in international relations, too, the Christian saying is valid: "The truth shall make you free" (John 8:32). (CM)

28. Peace on Earth — which man throughout the ages has so longed for and sought after — can never be established, never guaranteed, except by the diligent observance of the divinely established order. (PT, 1)

29. All men are united by their common origin and fellowship, their redemption by Christ, and their supernatural destiny. They are called to form one Christian family. (PT, 121)

30. The world will never be the dwelling place of peace, till peace has found a home in the heart of each and every man, till every man preserves in himself the order ordained by God to be preserved. (PT, 165)

31. I must, I will, become increasingly a man of intense prayer. (JS, 210)

32. I must . . . entrust myself at all times to divine providence. (JS, 311)

33. We did not debate, we talked; we did not discuss, but we became fond of each other! (JTP, 260)

34. Everything can be lost if men do not find some way to work together to save the peace. (IT, 63)

35. War has always been, and still is, a very grave evil; and whoever is familiar with the mind of Christ and his Gospel, and has the spirit of human and Christian brotherhood, can never sufficiently detest it. (PD, 96–97)

36. Nothing is more excellent than goodness. The human mind may look for other eminent gifts, but none of these can be compared with goodness. (PD, 161)

37. More important than any display of erudition are the hunger and thirst for the divine Word, because this is life to the soul, light to the mind, and the very breath of inspiration. (*PD*, 210)

38. There is no learning or wealth, there is no human power that is more effective than a good nature, a heart that is gentle, friendly, and patient. The good-hearted man may suffer mortifications and opposition, but he always wins through in the end because his goodness is love, and love is all-conquering. (*PD*, 271)

39. It is useless to admit that a man has a right to the necessities of life, unless we also do all in our power to supply him with means sufficient for his livelihood. (*PT*, 32)

40. When society is formed on a basis of rights and duties, men have an immediate grasp of spiritual and intellectual values, and have no difficulty in understanding what is meant by truth, justice, charity, and freedom. (*PT*, 45)

41. The attainment of the common good is the sole reason for the existence of civil authorities. (*PT*, 54)

42. All men . . . , private citizens as well as government officials, must love the truth sincerely if they are to attain that peace and harmony on which depends all real prosperity, public and private. (*APC*, 21)

43. All men . . . should turn their attention away from those things that divide and separate us, and should consider how they may be joined in mutual and just regard for one another's opinions and possessions. (*APC*, 29)

44. We have called nations, their rulers, and all classes of society to harmonious unity. Now we sincerely urge families to achieve and strengthen this unity within themselves. For unless peace, unity, and concord are present in domestic society, how can they exist in civil society? (*APC*, 50, 51)

45. Human life is sacred — all men must recognize that fact. (*MM*, 194)

46. One learns Christian behavior in social and economic matters by actual Christian action in those fields. (*MM*, 232)

47. No country has the right to take any action that would constitute an unjust oppression of other countries, or an unwarranted interference in their affairs. (*PT*, 120)

48. Every nation has its own genius, its own qualities, springing from the hidden roots of its being. (*MM*, 181)

49. It is not enough to assert that the right to own private property and the means of production is inherent in human nature. We must also insist on the extension of this right in practice to all classes of citizens. (*MM*, 113)

50. It is not enough merely to formulate a social doctrine. It must be translated into reality.... A purely theoretical instruction in man's social and economic obligations is inadequate. People must also be shown ways in which they can properly fulfill these obligations. (*MM*, 226, 230)